Go Mini Reference 2022
A Quick Guide to the Modern Go Programming Language for Busy Coders

Harry Yoon

Version 1.1.2, 2022-11-24

Copyright

Go Mini Reference:
A Quick Guide to the Modern Go Programming Language

Published: September 2022

Harry Yoon
San Diego, California

ISBN: 9798353247326

Preface

We are going through a Cambrian explosion of new programming languages. It seems like a new language is being created every day.

In the last decade or so, a new generation of programming languages were created, including Rust, Swift, Kotlin, Julia, and of course Go. They are now widely used alongside more traditional languages such as C/C++, Java, C#, Python, and Javascript, to name a few.

From 30,000 feet above, all these programming languages look more or less the same. As we go down, we can see some distinctions between imperative languages and functional languages. Although this distinction is becoming blurred as more imperative languages adopt various functional programming features, Go remains to be a quintessential imperative language.

As we go further down, we start to see some more details, and as we approach the ground, all programming languages look different, and appear rather unique in their own rights.

The Go programming language differentiates itself with a set of unique features, including the builtin concurrency support via goroutines. But, more importantly, Go stands out, among these hundreds of modern languages, in terms of its fundamental language design philosophy.

First of all, Go is a "minimalistic" language. Go is reminiscent of simple languages like Lua. The similarity between Go and Lua goes far deeper than their syntactic appearances. The minimalism is at the heart of the Go programming language design.

Second, Go values the stability of the language over anything else. This is in contrast with many other programming languages which are literally in the "arms race" for more and more features. Go is more like the C programming language in this regards, which has gone through absolutely minimal changes since its creation over four decades ago.

The recent introduction of generics, in Go 1.18, was an exception. Clearly, it was a necessary change. However, it opened up a can of worms as well. We will likely see some more (small and big) changes in the next few years or so before generics becomes a truly native part of the language.

Third, Go is a "batteries included" programming language when it comes to the standard libraries. Go is not necessarily unique in this respect. Languages like Python became widely popular partly due to this "batteries included" approach. Although there is a huge community of third party libraries and frameworks, Go gives you everything you need to get started in developing professional software without having to rely too much on external libraries.

This book is a "mini" language reference on the Go programming language. We go through all essential features of the modern Go programming language (as of 1.18 and 1.19) in this book. Although it is written as a reference, however, you can read it more or less from beginning to end and you should be able to get the overall picture of the Go language (but not necessarily all the gory details).

One thing to note is that there are a fair amount of cross references, unlike in the books written in a tutorial style, and if you have no prior experience with programming in Go, you may find it hard to read some parts of the book.

 This book is not an authoritative language reference. For that, we recommend the readers to refer to the official language specification.

Table of Contents

Chapter 1. Introduction

Go is a general-purpose programming language created by Google, and it was open-sourced a little over 10 years ago.

Go was originally designed as a "low level" systems programming language. It is now used broadly in many different systems and application areas including Web programming. It is currently one of the most widely used languages.

Go is a strongly typed language suitable for building a large scale system. Go is garbage-collected, which makes it easier to use by developers with a wide range of skill sets and which helps reduce many memory-related problems. Go has a native support for concurrent programming at the language level.

An executable Go program builds into a single standalone binary with no runtime (shared) library dependencies, making it easier to deploy across many different platforms. Any dependent Go libraries are imported during the build time as source code, not as pre-built shared libraries/binaries, reducing the chances of library conflicts.

Go is one of the simplest programming languages in terms of grammar, and it is one of the easiest to learn and use.

This book starts from the high level structure of a Go program, namely, packages. Then it describes how the Go programs are built and executed in the next chapter, Program Initialization and Execution. We briefly go through the *go* command and the module/workspace system.

In the Go programming language, the packages are used to organize the source code, and they are also the basic units of code sharing. In the standard go toolchain, one or more packages can be grouped into a module, e.g., for dependency management and versioning, etc., and one or more modules can be managed together using a workspace.

Go programs are written in Unicode. The Go compiler scans the characters in the input program, converts them first into a sequence of "tokens", and then parses it into an internal data structure that can be eventually converted to a machine code.

In the Lexical Elements chapter, we go through various low level aspects of the program code. In particular, we go through the basic elements, or tokens, like names/identifiers, keywords, comments, operators, and builtin type literals. Many programming languages have similar lexical structures, and this chapter can be skipped if you have experience with any C-style languages.

Every name in a Go program must be declared before use. That includes names for constants, variables, types, functions, methods, and the imported packages. We introduce the general concepts of declarations in the next chapter, and go through each of them in the following six chapters.

A constant declaration creates constants by binding names with constant expressions. Go supports boolean constants, numeric constants, and string constants.

Variables are used to hold values during program execution. A variable declaration binds names with expressions, and types, and it reserves storage for the named variables. We also go through a number of ways to allocate memory and initialize variables. For instance, the builtin new and make functions can be used for this purpose.

In the modern programming languages, types play crucial roles. Go is no exception. In the next chapter, Types, we go through the type system of Go.

- Go includes a set of builtin, or primitive, types that are found in most programming languages.

- Go has a support for creating composite types, such as arrays, slices, maps, and channels.

- `struct` can be used to create a structured data type.

- A type declaration allows creating a new type, or a type alias, from another type. Go now supports a generic type declaration.

- Go also supports pointer types, similar to C/C++, but with some restrictions. A pointer is an address to a variable.

An interface is a special kind of type. A (non-interface) type can *implicitly* "implement an interface" by implementing all methods declared in the given interface. A variable declared with an interface type can be used, at run time, for any of the types that implement this interface. This provides the runtime polymorphism in Go.

Since Go 1.18, interfaces can also be used as generic type constraints. In this usage, an interface represents a "type set" rather than a single polymorphic type. Go's generics requires type constraints for all generic type parameters. When any type can be used, one can use the interface type, any, which is an alias to `interface{}`.

As with any C-style programming languages, the function is one of the most important constructs in Go. (Just to be clear, using functions does not make Go a functional programming language, which seems to be a common misconception among beginning programmers.) Go's functions are rather similar to those of C, with some minor differences. In particular, Go functions can return zero, one, or *more* values.

Go also supports the method declaration syntax. A method in Go is just a function which is defined for a specific non-interface type called the "receiver". This way, functions can be organized in terms of their receivers' base types. Go now supports generic functions. A method can likewise be declared over a generic type.

Go also supports function literals, or anonymous functions, which are syntactically expressions rather than declarations.

Expressions and statements are the bread and butter of programming. Go supports most, if not all, of the common expressions found in C-style languages. For example,

- Constant expressions can be used to declare and initialize constant variables.

- Composite literals can be used to create a new value of a composite type such as arrays, slices, and maps.

- Index and slice expressions can be used to create, update, or otherwise manipulate, variables of collection types.

- Selector expressions are used for selecting fields and methods of a struct type.

- Function and method calls are expressions (regardless of whether they return any values).

- Type assertion expressions are used for runtime type assertion for polymorphic/interface types.

- The channel receive operation, e.g., `<-channel`, is an expression in Go.

- In addition, Go supports all common operation types, arithmetic, comparison, and logical, etc.

Likewise, Go includes all common statements generally found in other C-style programming languages. For instance,

- Assignments are used to bind values to variables.

- Many expressions can be used as statements. They are called expression statements.

- Unlike in C, postfix increment (`++`) and decrement (`--`) operations are statements in Go.

- The channel send operation, e.g., `channel<-`, is also a statement.

- Go supports `if`, `for`, and `switch` statements, with more or less the same semantics as in other C-style languages.

- Go supports switch-like `select` statement for channel operations.

- Go includes the common `continue`, `break`, and `return` statements.

- Because of the way Go's `switch` statement works, Go also includes the `fallthrough` statement.

- Go's rather unique `defer` statement can be used to "clean up" before a function returns.

- The `go` statement is used to create a new goroutine. Goroutines are used for concurrent programming in Go, among other things.

Go provides a minimal builtin support for error handling. By convention, functions return error values, or `nil` to indicate the non-error situation, as the last return value. The Go programming language includes a builtin `error` interface, which is commonly used for the error return type. In case of "unrecoverable" errors, the runtime panic is generally used in Go programs.

Go now finally has a generic type system. It is somewhat unfortunate that it took this long to have something so essential in statically and strongly typed languages like Go. But, despite the history, generics is not an ad-hoc addition to the type system. It is an integral part.

As stated, we go through generics *in the contexts* of type definitions and generic functions. However, if you are new to generics, this topic can be intimidating. Therefore, we include one bonus chapter to elaborate on generics. In particular, we provide an informal introduction to generics for beginners, followed by an example program implementing a generic stack data type, in the final chapter. This chapter is not part of the "language reference", and can be skipped.

Chapter 2. Packages

Go packages are the basic units of organization in Go programs. A Go program is constructed from one or more packages. A Go package, in turn, is constructed from one or more source code files.

In the current "standard" implementation, all source files of a package should be placed in the same directory. Source files in a given directory cannot belong to more than one package (with the exception of test file packages).

Therefore, the go programming construct, package, and the physical file system structure, *directory*, have a one-to-one correspondence with each other.

The source files belonging to a package declare *constants, types, variables, functions,* and *methods* of the package. They are unconditionally accessible in all files of the same package. A package provides a high-level scope in a Go program.

These "top-level" elements, constants, types, variables, functions, and methods, declared in a package may be exported, and they may be used in other packages in the same or another program (through the import mechanism).

2.1. Source File Organization

Each source file of a Go package consists of three parts, in the following order.

1. A package clause defining the package to which it belongs.

2. A set of import declarations that declare imported packages, if any.

3. A (possibly empty) set of top-level declarations of constants, types, variables, functions, and methods.

All top-level declarations belong to a `package`, and not to a specific source file where they are declared. One of the primary purposes of using multiple files would be for organizing the code in a given `package`, e.g., for readability, for maintainability, etc.

How the code in a `package` is divided into multiple source files is generally of no consequence to Go. One notable exception is the program initialization process. The language specification does not define the precise order. Different build systems may read the source files of a given package in different orders. The standard go toolchain reads the source files of a `package` in a lexical order using their file names.

The names introduced through `import declarations`, if any, may be referenced in the particular source file only, not across the `package`. This is referred to as the "source file scope".

2.2. Package Clause

The `package` clause is the first non-empty line in a source file, which declares the `package` name to which the file belongs. It is required.

A package clause starts with a keyword `package` followed by a *PackageName*.

```
package PackageName
```

The package name must be a valid non-blank identifier. The `package` clause is not a declaration. Its purpose is

- To identify the files belonging to the same package, and

- To specify the default package name for import declarations.

When a package is imported, the package name becomes, by default, an accessor for its contents.

A commonly used convention is that the package name is the base name of its source directory path. For example, the package for the source files in 'src/image/color' should have a name `color`, and not `image_color` or `ImageColor`, etc.

2.3. Import Declarations

A source file may include a set of `import` declarations, which states that the file containing the declaration depends on the functionality of the imported packages.

The imported packages are part of the program, and they are compiled on the local machine along with the program's source code.

An `import` declaration starts with a keyword `import` followed by one or more "import specifications", and it enables access to the exported identifiers of those packages specified in the `import` specification.

An `import` specification includes an "import path" that specifies the `package` to be imported. The `import` path can be optionally preceded by

- A period (`.`), or
- An identifier to be used for accessing the imported `package` within the importing source file.

The following `import` declaration imports a `package` in a directory "lib/math".

```
import    "lib/math"
```

If the imported package has the package clause `package`

mathematics, and if it includes an exported function declaration with a name Cosine, then the function can be referred to as mathematics.Cosine in the importing source file. If the imported package's package clause is package math instead, then the imported package name is math by default, and the Cosine function can be referred to as math.Cosine.

As stated, by convention, the last path segment of the package directory path is generally used as a package name. That is, it is typical, although not required, for the source files in a directory *.../lib/math* to belong to a package named math.

The imported package may be accessed with a different name, or alias, than the one declared in the imported source files.

For example, the following import declaration with an explicit name m allows the exported identifier Cosine to be referenced as m.Cosine within the importing source file.

```
import m "lib/math"
```

If a period (.) appears in that place, then all the exported identifiers declared in that package's package block will be automatically declared in the importing source file's file block. They must be accessed without a qualifier.

```
import . "lib/math"          ①
```

① Using the same example above, the exported name Cosine should be referred to simply as Cosine in the importing source file without any package qualifiers.

An import declaration can include more than one import specifications, in parentheses. Here's an example:

```
import (
    "lib/math"
    sci "lib/science"
)
```

It should be noted that the Go language specification does not precisely specify how the `import` path strings should be interpreted. It is implementation-dependent.

For local packages in the same module, for instance, an import path can be a relative path of the imported package with respect to the path of the importing source file. (Refer to the Modules chapter, however.) For packages remote to the computer, it can be a substring of the URL of the remote source code repository where the imported packages are found or otherwise identified. This is because the standard *go* build tool chain uses such conventions.

2.3.1. Importing for side effects

One special use case using the `import` declaration syntax is using the blank identifier (_) as a package name alias. For example,

```
import _ "lib/math"
```

In this case, although it appears syntactically to be an `import` declaration, it does not import the "lib/math" package's name (or, its exported names) into the source file. It is used solely for the purposes of side effects (e.g., for initialization). Otherwise, it is a no-op statement. Package initialization will be described in the next chapter.

2.4. Top-Level Statements

A source file typically includes, after the `package` clause and (optional)

`import` declarations, one or more declarations for constants, variables, types, functions, and methods.

These top-level statements essentially make up a package, and one or more packages make up a Go program.

The operating system starts an executable go program by calling a special entry function, `main`, in the special `main` package. This will be further discussed in the next chapter.

Chapter 3. Program Initialization and Execution

3.1. Program Execution

An executable Go program includes a special package, whose package name is `main`. A complete runnable program is created by linking this main package with all the dependent packages which it imports (local or remote), either directly or indirectly.

The main package must include a `mian` function declaration `main`, among other things. Program execution begins by initializing the main package, and the imported packages, and then by invoking the function `main()`, which may call other functions from the main package as well as from other imported packages, which in turn may import other packages, etc.

When the main function invocation ultimately returns, the program exits.

Go's `main` function takes no arguments and returns no value, unlike those of C or other C-style languages.

```
package main

func main() { /* ... */ }
```

The command line arguments, in a Go program, are passed in to the `main` functions via `os` environment variables, not as function arguments. Any special program exit code can be returned to the operating system via an explicit `os.Exit()` call.

The code of the main package can be included in one or more source files (in the same directory) just like other regular packages. The main package cannot be imported by other packages.

As a convention, the source file containing the main function in the main package is typically named *main.go*.

3.2. Initialization

3.2.1. Constants

Constants in Go are created at compile time, and hence they should be defined with constant expressions that can be evaluated by the compiler. Constants cannot be declared without their initial values.

Only the following builtin types (and, the types defined with these types) can be used for constants:

- bool,
- numbers (int and float types),
- runes, and
- strings.

3.2.2. Variables

Variables can be initialized just like constants. But, their values are computed at run time. Hence, a variable initializer can be a general expression, e.g., a function call, computable at run time. For example,

```
var (
    name = file.Name()
    size = file.Size()
)
```

3.2.3. Zero values

When no explicit initialization is provided, variables or values are given their default values. That is, all variables and values in Go are *always initialized*, either explicitly or implicitly with well-defined, definite values, unlike in many other programming languages.

For the variables of built-in types, their "zero values" are

- `false` for booleans,
- `0` for numeric types,
- `" "` for strings, and
- `nil` for functions, interfaces, slices, channels, and maps. Pointers' zero values are also `nil`.

For other composite types, e.g., arrays and structs, the initialization is done recursively. For example, each element of an array is set to "zero" if no value is specified.

3.2.4. Package initialization

If a package has any imports, then all imported packages, either directly or transitively, are initialized first before the package itself is initialized.

In a package, all package-level variables across one or more source code files are initialized through iterations.

In each iteration,

1. A variable is selected in the declaration order,
2. For a given variable,

   ◦ if the variable has no dependency on uninitialized variables, it is initialized,

   ◦ otherwise, it is skipped, and

3. If any new variable has been initialized in this iteration, then it goes to the next iteration.

4. Otherwise, the process terminates.

After this process is done, if there still remains a variable that has not been initialized, then the package is invalid.

3.2.5. The `init` functions

A package can have one or more `init` function which takes no arguments and returns no values.

```
package abc

func init() { /* ... */ }
```

Package-scope variables may also be initialized within these `init` functions, especially for those whose initializations cannot be expressed as simple declarations. Another common use of the `init` functions is to verify or repair correctness of the program state before real execution begins.

After all package level variable declarations are processed, the `init` functions are then called, in the order they appear in the source code files.

This completes the package initialization process.

3.3. The *go* Command

Although it is not part of the language specification per se, the *go* command is the de-facto standard tool in building Go programs. Here's the official doc:

- go command - cmd/go [https://pkg.go.dev/cmd/go]

Some of the most commonly used commands are *go get, go build, go run, go test,* and *go doc* as well as *go mod* and *go work,* as we will take a look in the next chapter.

One can use the *go help* command to get more information on each of these commands. For example,

```
$ go help build
usage: go build [-o output] [build flags] [packages]

Build compiles the packages named by the import paths,
along with their dependencies, ...
```

Chapter 4. Go Modules and Workspaces

As of 1.18+, Go now supports two ways to organize and manage related packages, *go modules* and a *go workspaces*.

 Modules and workspaces are not part of the Go language specification. They are specified by the current "standard" *go* toolchain.

4.1. Go Module

A module is a collection of related Go packages which are stored in a file tree with a *go.mod* file in its root directory. Go modules are the unit of source code sharing and versioning, and dependency management.

The *go.mod* file defines the module's module path, which is also the import path used for the root directory, and its dependency requirements. Each dependency requirement is written as a module path plus a specific semantic version.

The go command has builtin support for modules. For example, among other things,

- The go mod command can be used to initialize and manage a go module,

- The import specification can be based on the current module, and

- The go build command interprets the import specifications with respect to the module path.

4.1.1. The *go.mod* file

The *go.mod* file is line-oriented. Each line holds a *directive,* which is a pair of a "verb" and its arguments. The C++-style line comments (//) can be used in the *go.mod* file.

The following verbs are used

module   Defines the module path.

go   Sets the expected language version.

require   Requires a particular module at a given version or later,

exclude   Excludes a particular module version from use,

replace   Replaces a module path/version with a different module path/version.

retract   Indicates that a previously released version should not be used.

4.2. Go Workspace

The *go* command now supports the workspace mode. This can be enabled by putting a *go.work* file in the working directory or a parent directory, or by setting the *GOWORK* environment variable.

In the workspace mode, the *go.work* file will be used to determine the set of one or more main modules used as the roots for module resolution. The *go* command uses these modules for builds and related operations.

The *go* command has builtin support for workspaces. For example, among other things,

- The *go work* command can be used to create and manage a go workspace, and

- Various `go` commands can use the specified modules as root modules for builds and other operations.

4.2.1. The *go.work* file

The *go.work* file follows the same syntactical structure as the *go.mod* file. It is line-oriented, with each line holding a *directive*, made up of a verb followed by its arguments.

The allowed verbs are:

use   Specifies a module to be included in the workspace's set of main modules.

go   Specifies the version of Go which the file was written at.

replace Takes precedence over *replaces* in the go.mod files.

For example,

projects/banana-farm/go.work

```
go 1.19                  ①

use (                    ②
  ./producer
  ./consumer
  ./driver
)
```

① Go version.

② This workspace includes 3 modules.

projects/banana-farm/producer/go.mod

```
module gitlab.com/banana-farm/producer        ①

go 1.19                                        ②
```

① The `module` directive specifies the module path. The *go* command should be able to find this module from this path. (This example uses a fictitious path, for illustration.)

② The `go` directive specifies the Go version.

projects/banana-farm/producer/farmer.go

```
package producer

// ...
```

projects/banana-farm/consumer/go.mod

```
module gitlab.com/banana-farm/consumer        ①

go 1.19
```

① Another module included in the workspace.

projects/banana-farm/consumer/grocer.go

```
package consumer

// ...
```

projects/banana-farm/driver/go.mod

```
module driver                                  ①

go 1.19
```

```
require gitlab.com/banana-farm/producer v0.1.0          ②
require gitlab.com/banana-farm/consumer v0.1.0

replace gitlab.com/banana-farm/producer => ../producer   ③
replace gitlab.com/banana-farm/consumer => ../consumer
```

① The module that includes the `main` package. The module path is not significant since it will not be referenced.

② This module depends on two other modules. The `require` directive uses the same module paths used in the `go.mod` files for these modules.

③ The `replace` directive is used in this example to indicate that the *go* command should use the Go source files in the directories *projects/banana-farm/producer* and *projects/banana-farm/consumer* rather than those from the remote git repositories.

projects/banana-farm/driver/main.go

```
package main

import (
  "gitlab.com/banana-farm/producer"          ①
  "gitlab.com/banana-farm/producer/farm"     ②
  "gitlab.com/banana-farm/consumer"          ③
)

// Produce and consume bananas...
```

① This example *main.go* file depends on the `producer` package in the root directory of the producer module.

② For illustration, the producer module happens to include another package `farm` in the *projects/banana-farm/producer/farm* folder.

③ In all these 3 import specifications, the source files are fetched from the local file system when building the main package thanks to the `replace` directives in the *driver/go.mod* file.

Note that, in this particular example, the `go.work` file is located in the parent directory of all three modules, producer, consumer, and driver. But, in general, this is not required. The go workspace can be created anywhere, and it can include modules from anywhere using the `use` directive.

Another thing to note is that each module in a workspace can, and typically does, include a main package of its own. A module can belong to more than one workspaces.

Chapter 5. Lexical Elements

5.1. Comments

Go supports two kinds of comments.

C++-Style Line Comments

A line comment starts with the character sequence `//` and it continues until just before the end of the line. This is the form that is more commonly used.

C-Style Block Comments

A block comment starts with the character sequence `/*` and it stops after the first subsequent character sequence `*/`. Block comments are typically used for package doc comments or to "comment out" some large part of code.

In Go programs, comments serve primarily as program documentation. The *go doc* command processes Go source files to extract documentation about the contents of the package.

5.2. Semicolons

Go's formal grammar uses semicolons to terminate statements like in most C-style languages. However, those semicolons do not generally appear in the Go source code.

Lexer automatically adds semicolons ; at the end of a line if the final token is one of the following:

- An identifier,

- An integer, floating-point, imaginary, rune, or string literal,

- One of the keywords `break`, `continue`, `fallthrough`, or `return`, or

- One of the operators and punctuation ++, --,),], or }.

Lexer also adds a semicolon, if missing, before a closing) or }.

5.3. Tokens

There are four classes of lexical tokens in the Go language:

- Identifiers,
- Keywords,
- Operators and punctuation, and
- Literals.

5.4. Identifiers

An identifier is a name for program entities such as variables and types. An identifier comprises one or more letters and digits, and its first character must be a letter.

5.5. Keywords

The keywords are reserved, and they may not be used as identifiers in a Go program.

```
break       default      func     interface   select
case        defer        go       map         struct
chan        else         goto     package     switch
const       fallthrough  if       range       type
continue    for          import   return      var
```

5.6. Operators and Punctuation

The following characters and character sequences represent operators and punctuation:

+	&	+=	&=	&&	==	!=	(	)
-	|	-=	|=	||	<	<=	[	]
*	^	*=	^=	<-	>	>=	{	}
/	<<	/=	<<=	++	=	:=	,	;
%	>>	%=	>>=	--	!	...	.	:
	&^		&^=		~			

5.7. Literals

Go supports the following builtin type literals, which are constant expressions:

- Integer literals,
- Floating-point literals,
- Imaginary literals,
- Rune literals, and
- String literals.

Other literal types, array, slice, and map literals, are discussed later in the book.

5.7.1. Integer literals

An integer literal represents an integer constant.

- A binary integer literal starts with the prefix 0b or 0B and it is followed by one or more digits (0 - 9) or non-consecutive/non-trailing underscores (_).

- An octal integer literal starts with `0`, `0o`, or `0O` and is followed by one or more digits or non-consecutive/non-trailing underscores.

- A hexadecimal integer literal is `0x` or `0X` followed by one or more digits or non-consecutive/non-trailing underscores.

- All other sequences of digits and non-consecutive underscores (except at the starting and ending positions), including `0`, represent decimal integer literals.

Underscores are ignored when evaluating the integer literals. For instance, `1_000_000` and `1000000` are the same integer constants, whose values are `1000000`.

5.7.2. Floating-point literals

A floating-point literal represents a floating-point number constant, either in decimal or hexadecimal notations. A floating point literal comprises an integer part, a decimal point (`.`), a fractional part, and an optional exponent part (using `e` or `E` for decimals or using `p` or `P` for hexadecimals). One of the integer and fractional parts, but not both, can be omitted if their value is `0`.

As with integer literals, non-consecutive underscores (`_`) can be used to between successive digits, or between the hexadecimal prefix and the following digit, for floating point literals without affecting their values.

```
.1_2_3              ①
0x20.               ②
10.5e2              ③
0x_f.P1             ④
```

① A decimal floating point literal. This is equivalent to `0.123`, etc.

② A hexadecimal floating point literal. This is equivalent to `0x20.0`, etc.

③ A decimal floating point literal. This is equivalent to `1050.`, etc.

④ A hexadecimal floating point literal. This is equivalent to `0xf0.0`, etc.

5.7.3. Imaginary literals

An imaginary literal comprises an integer or floating-point literal followed by `i`, and it represents an imaginary number constant.

```
5i              ①
.5e12i          ②
5 + i           ③
```

① An imaginary number literal, whose value is `5i == 5 * i`.

② An imaginary number literal, `50.i == 50. * i`.

③ A complex number expression, the addition of an integer constant `5` and `1 * i`.

5.7.4. Rune literals

A rune is an integer value corresponding to a single Unicode code point. A rune literal is syntactically represented with one or more characters, except for newlines and single quotes, enclosed in single quotes.

- A quoted single character represents the Unicode value of the character.

- A quoted special escape sequence, a backslash (\) followed a single character, represents the Unicode value of that escape sequence.

- A quoted multi-character sequence starting with a backslash in one of the following four formats represents the Unicode integer value in the specified base, as long as it corresponds to a valid Unicode code point:

- ◦ \ followed by *three* octal digits,

- ◦ \x followed by *two* hexadecimal digits,

- ◦ \u followed by *four* hexadecimal digits, and

- ◦ \U followed by *eight* hexadecimal digits (for two Unicode code points, e.g., for non-BMP characters).

```
'A'                     ①
'\n'                    ②
'\007'                  ③
'x24'                   ④
'\u002A'                ⑤
'\U000000e4'            ⑥
```

① A rune literal representing the English uppercase letter A.

② A rune literal representing the newline character.

③ A rune literal representing the bell character in the octal number representation.

④ A rune literal representing the dollar symbol. The same as '$'.

⑤ A rune literal representing the asterisk symbol. The same as '*'.

⑥ A rune literal representing the character ä, a-dieresis. The same as 'ä'.

5.7.5. String literals

A string in Go is a sequence of (Unicode) characters There are two forms of string literals:

- Raw string literals, and

- Interpreted string literals.

Raw string literals

- Raw string literals are **character sequences** between back quotes, as in `` `foo` ``.

- Within the quotes, any character may appear except back quote.

- The value of a raw string literal is the string composed of the uninterpreted characters between the quotes.

Interpreted string literals

- Interpreted string literals are character sequences between double quotes, as in `"bar"`.

- Within the quotes, any character may appear except newline and unescaped double quote.

- The text between the quotes forms the value of the literal, with backslash escapes interpreted as they are in rune literals.

Chapter 6. Declarations and Scope

6.1. Declarations

A *declaration* binds a (non-blank) identifier to a constant, variable, type, function, method, label, or an imported package.

Every non-blank identifier in a Go program must be declared before use. No identifier may be declared twice in the same block, or across file and package blocks.

An identifier declared in a block may be redeclared in an inner block. While the identifier of the inner declaration is in scope, it denotes the entity declared by the inner declaration. This is known as "shadowing".

6.2. Top-Level Declarations

A Go package primarily includes a number of top level declarations (other than the package clause and import statements, if any, needed in each source file).

The following are considered top-level declarations in Go:

- Constant declarations,
- Variable declarations,
- Type/Interface declarations,
- Function declarations, and
- Method declarations.

Function and method declarations can only be used in the top-level package scope. Constant, variable, and (interface and non-interface) type declarations, as well as label declarations, can be used within a non-file/package block, such as inside a function definition.

6.3. Blocks

Statements control program execution in Go. A block is a sequence of zero, one, or more statements. Blocks can nest, and they affect scoping.

Statements can be explicitly grouped into a block using a pair of curly braces. Unlike in some C-style languages, the enclosing curly braces are required for all (explicit) blocks. They cannot be omitted, even for single-statement blocks.

In addition, the Go grammar considers the following an implicit block without requiring curly braces:

- The "universe block" including all source code from all packages in a program.
- A package block containing all Go source text for each package.
- A file block containing all Go source text in a given source code file.
- Each `if`, `for`, and `switch` statement.
- Each `case`/`default` clause in a `switch` or `select` statement.

6.4. Scoping

Go is lexically scoped using (explicit or implicit) blocks. The scope of an identifier is the extent of source text in which the identifier denotes the declared constant, variable, type, function, method, label, or imported package.

- The scope of a Go predeclared identifier (e.g., `int`, `true`) is the universe block.
- The scope of an identifier denoting a constant, variable, type, or

function declared at a package level (e.g., outside a function definition) is the package block.

- The scope of an imported package name is the file block. Except for this case, a file block is not considered a distinct block from a package block for the purposes of scoping.

- The scope of an identifier denoting a method receiver, function parameter, or return variable is the function body.

- The scope of a constant or variable identifier declared inside a function begins at the end of the declaration statement and it ends at the end of the innermost containing block.

- The scope of a type identifier declared inside a function begins at the identifier in the type declaration statement and it ends at the end of the innermost containing block.

6.5. Label Scopes

Labels are declared by labeled statements and are used in the break, continue, and goto statements.

In contrast to other identifiers, labels are not block scoped, and they do not conflict with non-label identifiers.

Labels can only be declared within a function/method definition. The scope of a label is the body of the function in which it is declared (which can possibly include a region preceding the labeled statement), and it excludes the body of any nested function. Defining a label that is not used in the scope is a syntactic error.

6.6. Blank Identifier

The blank identifier (_) serves as an anonymous placeholder in place of a regular identifier in a declaration.

The blank identifier can be assigned or declared with any expression of any type. The expression is evaluated, but the result is ignored. The blank identifier cannot be referenced.

6.7. Exporting Identifiers

Identifiers in a package are not exported by default.

An identifier declared in a package block is exported if the first character of the identifier's name is a Unicode upper case letter. Likewise, the name of a field or method of a type that is exported is also exported if the first character of the name is an upper case letter. Exported identifiers can be accessed from another package.

Go has no other mechanism for access controls, unlike in some other modern programming languages.

Chapter 7. Constants

7.1. Constant Declarations

A constant declaration creates constants with constant expressions by binding one or more lists of identifiers with the corresponding lists of values. The number of identifiers in each list on the left hand side must be equal to the number of expressions in the corresponding list on the right hand side.

For example,

```
const KlingonPi, RomulanPi = 31.4, 314.2
```

```
const (
    UniversalZero          = 0
    KlingonOne, RomulanOne = 10.0, 100
)
```

The type of identifiers in each list can be explicitly specified, in which case all expressions must be assignable to that type. Otherwise, the constants take the individual types of the corresponding expressions.

```
const (
    KlingonTen, RomulanTen            float32 = 100.0, 1000
①
    KlingonHundred, RomulanHundred            = 1000.0, 10_000
②
)
```

① Both KlingonTen and RomulanTen are of the type float32.

② `KlingonHundred` and `RomulanHundred` are of the "untyped float" and "untyped int" types, respectively.

7.2. Constants

Go supports boolean constants, numeric constants (rune, integer, floating-point, and complex numbers), and string constants.

The boolean truth values are represented by the predeclared constants `true` and `false`. The predeclared identifier `iota` denotes an untyped integer constant.

Constants may be typed or untyped. Literal constants, `true`, `false`, `iota`, and certain constant expressions containing only untyped constant operands are untyped.

When untyped constants are assigned to a typed variable without explicit types, e.g., in a short variable declaration such as `i := 0`, they are converted to their corresponding default types:

Boolean constants	`bool`
Rune constants	`rune`
String constants	`string`
Integer constants	`int`
Floating point constants	`float64`
Complex numbers	`complex128`

7.3. Iota

Within each constant declaration, the predeclared identifier `iota` represents successive untyped integer constants, starting at 0 on the first identifier-expression lists. iota is generally used to construct a set of related constants (similar to enums in some other programming languages).

```
const (
    r, g, b = iota, iota + 10, iota + 20    ①
    y       = iota                          ②
    _                                       ③
    k                                       ④
)
```

① r == 0, g == 10, and b == 20. Note that all iota's on this line have the same value 0.

② y == 1. iota has been incremented by 1.

③ This line is the same as _ = iota (from y = iota above), which is discarded. The value of iota is 2 on this line.

④ Likewise, the value of k is iota (from the line y = iota) since it is not explicitly specified. iota is 3 at this point, and hence k == 3.

Chapter 8. Variables

A variable is a location in memory for holding a value. The set of permissible values for a given variable is determined by its type.

When a variable is referred to in an expression, its value is returned. The value of a variable is the most recent value assigned to the variable. If a variable has not yet been explicitly assigned a value, its value is the "zero value" for its type.

A variable declaration reserves storage for a named variable at build time. Likewise, a function declaration and function literal reserves storage for function parameters and results. The "static type" of a variable is the type given in its declaration.

A variables of an interface type also has a distinct "dynamic type", which is the concrete type of the value assigned to the variable at run time.

8.1. Variable Declarations

A variable declaration binds a list of identifiers to the values of the corresponding list of expressions, and gives each identifier a type, or static type, and an (explicit or implicit) initial value.

```
var speed, direction float64        ①
```

① Both `speed` and `direction` are of type `float64` and they are initialized with `0.0`.

```
var (
    NumGames int32                      ①
    NumWins, NumLosses = 0, 10          ②
```

```
    )
```

① `NumGames` is of the `int32` type and it is initialized with `0`.

② `NumWins` and `NumLosses` are of the `int` type and their initial values are `0` and `10`, respectively.

8.2. Short Variable Declarations

A short variable declaration is a shorthand for a (non-parenthesized) variable declaration with initializer expressions, but without explicit type specifications.

A short variable declaration uses the `:=` operator instead of the regular assignment operator `=`. They can be used only in a function block, or within a local block in a function block, to declare local variables.

For example,

```
func doNothing() {
    var a0, a1 = 0.0, 1.0
    b0, b1 := 0.0, 1.0
    println(a0, a1, b0, b1)
}
```

In this example, all 4 variables are of the `float64` type. The values of `a0` and `b0` are `0.0`, and the values of `a1` and `b1` are `1.0`, after executing each of these statements.

8.3. Variable Re-Declarations

Identifiers in Go cannot be generally redeclared within the same block. When a short multi-variable declaration syntax is used, however, a variable can be redeclared as long as

- That variable was declared with the same type earlier in the same block, and

- The short variable declaration statement includes at least one new non-blank identifier.

For instance,

```
func doSomething() {
    var c0 int = 10
    println(c0)
    c0, c1 := 20, 40
    println(c0, c1)
}
```

In this example, the variable c0 appears to be declared twice, first through the regular var declaration with the initial value 10, and second through the short variable declaration with the new initial value 20. Because c1 is declared for the first time in this statement, the redeclaration of c0 is allowed.

8.4. The Builtin new Function

Go has a built-in function, new, that allocates memory for a given type T, including struct types. But unlike the "new" functions/operators in some other languages, it does not *initialize* the memory. It only *zeros* it.

That is, new(T) allocates zeroed storage for a new item of type T and returns its address, a value of type *T. In Go, this is called a pointer, which points to the newly allocated zero value of type T. In case of a struct type T, new(T) and a composite literal expression &T{} (with no field initializers) are equivalent.

8.5. The Builtin make Function

In contrast to new(T), the builtin function make(T, args) is only used to create slices, maps, and channels. The make function allocates memory and it returns an *initialized* value of type T (not *T).

For slices, maps, and channels, make initializes the internal data structure and prepares the value for use.

For example, make([]int, 10, 100) allocates an array of 100 ints and then creates a slice structure with length 10 and a capacity of 100 pointing at the first 10 elements of the array.

In contrast, new([]int) returns a pointer to a newly allocated, zeroed slice structure, that is, a pointer to a nil slice value.

Chapter 9. Types

9.1. Types (And Generic Types)

A *type* essentially defines

- A set of all possible values (for the given type), and

- The operations allowed on those values.

Types are not mutually exclusive. That is, a value can belong to more than one types. In particular, in Go, a value can belong to at most one non-interface type (across compile and run time), and it can belong to zero, one, or more interface types at the same time. Furthermore, a value has at least one type at compile type (known as a "static type").

The Go language includes a number of predeclared types:

```
any bool byte comparable
complex64 complex128 error float32 float64
int int8 int16 int32 int64 rune string
uint uint8 uint16 uint32 uint64 uintptr
```

New types may be created, e.g., using composite type literals:

```
array, struct, pointer, function, interface, slice, map,
channel
```

A type can be anonymous. Or, a type can be denoted by an explicit type name followed by an optional type argument.

Go also supports parameterized types (since Go 1.18). A named type declaration can be parameterized with a type parameter, which essentially declares a set of possible types. A named type with a type parameter is called a generic type.

For instance, this example declares a generic struct type Node with type parameter E, which can be used for creating a (generic) linked list data structure.

```
type Node[E any] struct {
    Item E
    Next *Node[E]
}
```

E is constrained to be of type any, in this example. any is a predeclared type alias for interface {}. Every value in Go is of type any. Hence, any type can be used to define a concrete type of Node. For instance, Node[int] is a valid type as well as Node[string], and so forth.

9.2. Method Sets

Every type has a (possibly empty) "method set" associated with it. The method set of a type determines what interfaces the type (implicitly) implements and what methods can be called using a receiver of that type. In a method set, each method must have a unique non-blank method name.

- The method set of an interface type is its interface.
- The method set of a non-interface type T consists of all methods declared with receiver type T.
- The method set of the corresponding pointer type *T is the set of all methods declared with both receivers *T and T
- Any other type has an empty method set.

9.3. Underlying Types

Each type T has an "underlying type":

- If T is one of the predeclared types, then the corresponding underlying type is T itself.

- Otherwise, T's underlying type is the underlying type of the type to which T refers in its type definition or alias declaration.

- The underlying type of a generic type parameter is the underlying (interface) type of its type constraint interface.

9.4. Type Declarations

A type declaration (using the keyword type) binds a list of identifiers (type names) to a list of types. There are two kinds of type declarations: alias declarations and type definitions.

9.4.1. Alias declarations

A type alias declaration, which uses an assignment-like syntax, after the type keyword, binds an identifier(s) to the given (existing) type(s).

Within the scope of the identifier, it serves as an alias for the type. For example,

```
type (                    ①
    Rank     = uint8      ②
    Suit     = rune       ③
)
```

① The parentheses are required when more than one types/aliases are declared in one statement.

② Rank and uint8 are identical types. Multiple alias declarations are syntactically to be separated by semicolons (;), but they are normally omitted.

③ Suit is an alias to rune, which is in turn a (predeclared) alias to int32. Suit, rune, and int32 are all identical types in the given scope.

9.4.2. Type definitions

Based on another type (named or otherwise), a type definition creates a new, distinct named type with the same underlying type and operations as the given type. The identifier in the type definition serves as the name of the new type.

The new type created this way is called a *defined type*. It is different from any other type, including the type it is created from. In particular, it does *not* inherit any methods bound to the given type. Methods may be associated with a new defined type.

The type definition uses a similar syntax:

- The type keyword, followed by

- A list of *name type* pairs, separated by semicolons, enclosed in parentheses.

When there is only one *name type* pair, the parentheses are not required.

```
type Rank uint8              ①
```

① Rank is a new type distinct from uint8, unlike in the earlier alias declaration example. Type definitions and alias declarations are syntactically different by the presence/absence of the equal (=) sign. The underlying type of Rank is uint8 in this example.

A named new type can be created from an anonymous type as well. For example,

```
type (
    Point struct{ x, y int32 }      ①
    Coord Point                     ②
)
```

① Point and struct{ x, y int32 } are different and distinct types. Point is, however, structurally identical to the specified (anonymous) type, an anonymous struct struct{ x, y int32 } in this example.

② Coord and Point and struct{ x, y int32 } are all different types.

Another example, where a new type is created based on an interface type:

```
type Mover interface {          ①
    Move() bool
}
```

① Mover and interface{ Move() } are different types. But, the method set of Mover includes a method Move() bool.

A generic type can be created using the type definition syntax (but not through the alias declarations). Generic types are explained next.

9.5. Type Parameter Lists

Go allows creating generic types, and generic functions, with type parameters. Generic types can also be used in the receiver specification of a method declaration.

In type definitions and function definitions, the generic type parameters appear between brackets ([ ]) after the declared name,

- Before the target type, in case of type definitions, and
- Before the function's arguments, in case of function definitions.

For example,

```
type List[T any] struct {            ①
    Items []T                        ②
}
```

① A type parameter, T in this example, is introduced after the new type name, List.

② The type parameter can be used in the struct definition as if it is a concrete type.

```
func Cons[T any]                     ①
   (head T, list List[T])            ②
   List[T] {                         ③
   return List[T] {                  ④
      Items: append([head], list.Items...)
   }
}
```

① A type parameter T is introduced after the function name, Cons.

② The type parameter can be used in the function parameter list.

③ It can be used in the function return value type.

④ And, it can be used in the function body. The example code is for demonstration purposes only.

Syntactically, a generic type parameter list is one or more type parameters, and their corresponding type constraints, enclosed in square brackets. Parameters are comma-separated.

The type parameter names, such as T or E, are placeholder identifiers, and they must be unique across all parameters in a list. When a generic type or function, or a receiver type of a method, is instantiated/used, the generic type parameter is replaced with a concrete type argument.

9.5.1. Type constraints

Type constraints are specifications that constrain the allowed types of the given type parameters.

More specifically, a type constraint in Go is an interface that defines the set of permissible types for the corresponding type parameter. It effectively specifies the operations to be supported by values of that type parameter.

A type constraint is always required in Go, even if it is just any. For instance,

```
[T any]                              ①
[C comparable]                       ②
[D ~[]E, E comparable]               ③
[S interface{ string | ~[]byte }]    ④
[_ any]                              ⑤
```

① T is essentially unconstrained.

② comparable is an interface defined in the standard library.

③ The first type parameter D uses the second type parameter E in its type constraint.

④ An anonymous interface definition is used as a type constraint.

⑤ A blank identifier can be used as a type parameter.

Any interface can be used as a generic type constraint. Go interfaces are explained in more detail later in the book.

`any`

The predeclared name `any`, first introduced in Go 1.18, is an alias for `interface{}`. The type constraint of `any` means that there is no constraint for the respective type parameter.

`comparable`

The predeclared interface type `comparable`, first introduced in Go 1.18, does not include any specific methods. The sole purpose of this special interface is to denote the set of all concrete (non-interface) types that are "comparable".

A type T is considered to implement `comparable` if:

- T is an non-interface type and T supports the operations `==` and `!=`; or

- T is an interface type and each type in T's type set implements `comparable`.

9.6. Predeclared Types

Go includes a number of predeclared named types.

9.6.1. Interface types

`any`

It is an alias to `interface{}`. All non-interface types in Go, builtin or user-defined, implements `any`.

`comparable`

It denote the set of all non-interface types that are "comparable". The `comparable` interface is primarily used as a type parameter constraint in generic definitions.

error

> The predeclared type `error` includes one method, `Error() string`.
> Error handling is discussed at the end of the book.

9.6.2. Boolean types

Go predeclares a boolean type, `bool`, which represents the set of two
logical values, `true` and `false`. A new named boolean type can be
created using a type definition, just like any other types. For example,

```
type ToBeOrNotToBe bool
```

9.6.3. Numeric types

Go includes a set of predefined numeric types to represent the set of
integer, floating-point, and complex values.

The architecture-independent numeric types are:

```
uint8       the set of all unsigned  8-bit integers (0 to 255)
uint16      the set of all unsigned 16-bit integers (0 to
65535)
uint32      the set of all unsigned 32-bit integers (0 to
4294967295)
uint64      the set of all unsigned 64-bit integers (0 to
18446744073709551615)

int8        the set of all signed  8-bit integers (-128 to
127)
int16       the set of all signed 16-bit integers (-32768 to
32767)
int32       the set of all signed 32-bit integers (-2147483648
to 2147483647)
```

```
int64        the set of all signed 64-bit integers (-
9223372036854775808 to 9223372036854775807)

float32      the set of all IEEE-754 32-bit floating-point
numbers
float64      the set of all IEEE-754 64-bit floating-point
numbers

complex64    the set of all complex numbers with float32 real
and imaginary parts
complex128   the set of all complex numbers with float64 real
and imaginary parts
```

There is also a set of predeclared numeric types with implementation-specific sizes:

```
uint     either 32 or 64 bits
int      same size as uint
uintptr  an unsigned integer large enough to store the
uninterpreted bits of a pointer value
```

These numeric types are *defined types*, and they are all distinct from each other. Explicit conversions are required when different numeric types are mixed in an expression or assignment.

In addition, Go includes two predeclared type aliases, `byte` and `rune`:

```
byte        alias for uint8
rune        alias for int32
```

9.6.4. String types

The predefined `string` type represents the set of string values. A string value is a (possibly empty) sequence of bytes. The number of bytes is called the length of the string, which can be found using the built-in function `len`.

Strings are *immutable*. That is, once created, the contents of the string cannot be changed. The internal bytes of a string `s` can be accessed (read-only) by integer indices, `0` through `len(s)-1`.

- A `string` in Go has a dual nature. It is physically a sequence of bytes, and it is logically a sequence of runes at the same time. A `string` can always be converted to `[]byte` whereas not every sequence of bytes is a valid `string`.

- The string literal syntax is discussed in the lexical analysis chapter.

- The string concatenation is discussed in the context of arithmetic expressions.

- The `append function` can be used to create a *new* string from existing strings.

9.7. Array Types

An array type is a composite type comprising a sequence of elements of a single type (known as the "element type"). The elements of an array are stored in consecutive space in memory, and they can be indexed.

An array type is denoted with the following syntax:

```
[ Length ] ElementType
```

 Note that all builtin collection types, `array`, `slice`, and `map`, as well as `chan`, are essentially generic types although the (new) generic type syntax is not used.

An array type can be defined by specifying the number of elements in square brackets followed by the array's element type.

The number of elements is called the length of the array, and it is non-negative. The length is part of the array's type. The length of an array type should be specified with a constant expression.

As an example, the following type definition creates a named type, `Ints`, based on an array type, `[10]int32`, whose element type is `int32` and whose length is `10`.

```
type Ints [10]int32
```

You can create a variable of an array type:

```
var arr [100]bool
```

The variable `arr` is of the type `[100]bool` comprising 100 `bool` elements in a consecutive memory space. All elements are initialized with `false` (the zero value of the `bool` type).

9.7.1. Indexing

The elements of an array `a` can be addressed by integer indices `0` through `len(a)-1`. The indices in Go are of the architecture-dependent `int` type.

Indexing and slicing are further discussed in the later chapters, index expressions and slice expressions.

9.7.2. Array literal

An array composite literal is used to create a new instance of a specified array type. For instance,

```
arr := [...]int{1, 2, 3}            ①
```

① An array literal that creates a 3 element `int` array is used to initialize the variable `arr`. The length of the array literal need not be explicitly specified (that is, one can use … in place of the exact length). The type of `arr` is `[3]int`.

The composite literals are explained in more detail in the composite literal expressions chapter.

9.7.3. Multi-dimensional arrays

Go does not have true multi-dimensional arrays. Array types are always one-dimensional. However, an array type can be composed with an array element type, whose element type can be another array type, etc.

9.8. Slice Types

Slice types are another class of composite types in Go, built from other types. A slice is defined over an underlying array, and it represents a contiguous segment of that array. A slice type denotes the set of all possible slices over the arrays of its element type.

A slice, once initialized, is always associated with an underlying array that holds its elements. A slice therefore shares storage with its array and with other slices of the same array.

The number of elements in a slice `s` is called its length, `len(s)`. The elements of an array `a` can be accessed through a slice `s` over a, e.g., using `s := a[:]`. The integer indices runs from 0 to `len(s)-1`.

The length of the underlying array, in this example, is called the *capacity* of the slice. The capacity of a slice over an array, in general, can be equal to, or less than, the length of the underlying array.

The index and slice operations over slices are discussed later.

A slice type can be defined using an empty pair of square brackets. For instance,

```
type s1 []string
```

The named type s1 is defined based on an anonymous slice type []string. Note that the []string type represents *all* possible slices over *all* different array types whose element type is string, including [10]string, [100]string, etc.

```
var i1 []int
```

In this example, the variable i1 is of the []int slice type. The value of an uninitialized variable of a slice type is nil.

9.8.1. Slice construction

Slice literals

A slice composite literal can be used to create a new slice, in a similar way that an array literal is used to create a new array. For example,

```
slice := []int{1, 2, 3}              ①
```

① The slice literal on the right hand side of the short variable declaration creates a 3 element int slice with the underlying array [3]int{1, 2, 3}. The type of slice is []int.

Slice expressions

A new slice can also be created from an existing array or slice, using the slice expression, which is discussed later in the book.

The make function

In addition, a (zero-initialized) slice can be created using the builtin
function make. For example,

```
s1 := make([]bool, 10)          ①
s2 := make([]string, 5, 100)    ②
```

① The slice s1 of type []bool has length 10 and capacity 10. All its
   elements are initialized with false (the zero value of the bool
   type).

② s2 has a type []string. Its length and capacity are 5 and 100,
   respectively. Each element of its underlying array, of type
   [100]string, is initialized with "".

9.8.2. The append function

The builtin function append has the following function signature:

```
func (slice []T, elements ...T) []T      ①
```

① Although the function is technically not a generic function, it is
   nonetheless defined over a type parameter T. The ... syntax signifies
   that it is a variadic function.

The append function appends elements to the end of slice. For
example,

```
s1 := []int{2, 4}
s1 = append(s1, 6, 8)              ①
s1 = append(s1, []int{10, 12}...)  ②
```

① The value of s1 at this point is []int{2, 4, 6, 8}. Reusing the same variable for the returned value from the append function is idiomatic.

② The value of s1 after the assignment is []int{2, 4, 6, 8, 10, 12}.

Note that the underlying array of the resulting slice can be different from that of theinput slice. The append function uses the same underlying array if the input slice's capacity is big enough to accommodate the new elements. Otherwise, it creates a new underlying array and uses it for the resulting slice.

9.9. Map Types

A map is a group of zero or more values or variables of one specified type ("element type") indexed by a set of keys of another specified type ("key type").

- The builtin len function returns the number of map elements (" length").

- Elements in a map are unordered.

- All keys must be unique.

A map type is a composite type comprising the key type and the element type. Syntactically, a map type is denoted as follows:

```
map [ KeyType ] ElementType
```

In the following type definition,

```
type Timezone map[string]int
```

A new named `map` type `Timezone` is created, whose key and element types are `string` and `int`, respectively. Likewise,

```
var daysOfMonth map[rune]uint8
```

In this example, the `daysOfMonth` variable is of an anonymous `map` type `map[rune]uint8`, whose key and element types are `rune` and `uint8`, respectively. Since `rune` is an alias to `int32`, this type is equivalent to `map[int32]uint8`.

9.9.1. Key types

The types which do not fully support the comparison operators `==` and `!=`, including functions, maps, and slices, cannot be used as a key type of a map.

If the key type is an interface type, these comparison operators must be defined for the dynamic key type at run time. Otherwise, it will cause a run-time panic.

Note that, since Go 1.18, the predeclared `comparable` interface can be used to constrain permissible key types.

9.9.2. Map construction

The `make` function

A new, empty map value can be created using the built-in `make` function. The `make` function takes a specific `map` type as an argument. An optional capacity hint can be provided as a second argument.

For example,

```
var m1 = make(map[string]int)          ①
```

```
var m2 = make(map[int]byte, 100)        ②
```

① m1 is an empty map of type `map[string]int`.

② m2 is an empty map of type `map[int]byte`, whose initial capacity is `100`.

Map literals

A `map` can also be constructed using a composite literal syntax with colon-separated key-value pairs. For instance,

```
var daysOfMonth = map[string]int {
    "January": 31,
    "February": 28,
    "March": 31,
}
```

In this example, the variable `daysOfMonth` has type `map[string]int` and it has 3 elements.

9.9.3. Indexing

Each element can be addressed using the index notation. For instance, `daysOfMonth["January"]` evaluates to `31` (of type `int`) in the above example.

The index expression can also be used on the left hand side of assignment statement. For example,

```
daysOfMonth["February"] = 29
```

A new element can also be added this way:

```
daysOfMonth["April"] = 30
```

At this point, `len(daysOfMonth)` will return 4.

One can iterate over all elements in a map, e.g., using the for - range statement. For instance, using the same example,

```
for k, v := range daysOfMonth {
    fmt.PrintLn(k, "\t", v)
}
```

This will print out the following output:

```
January    31
February   29
March      31
April      30
```

9.9.4. Deleting elements

Elements of a map may also be removed using the builtin delete function. For example,

```
delete(daysOfMonth, "February")
```

`len(daysOfMonth)` at this point will return 3.

9.10. Channel Types

A channel holds values of a specific element type that can be accessed across multiple concurrently executing functions. A function can "send" and/or "receive" values to/from a channel.

A `chan T` type specifies its element type `T` and optionally the "direction". The `<-` operator specifies the channel direction, send (`chan<-`) or receive (`<-chan`). If no direction is given, the channels of a given `chan` type are bidirectional. That is, they can be read from and written to.

The zero value of a `chan` type is `nil`.

The following type definition creates a new named `chan` type:

```
type IntBuf chan int
```

The `IntBuf` type defines a set of bidirectional channels with `int` as its element type. In contrast, `chan<- int` and `<-chan int` represent channels for only sending and only receiving `int` values, respectively.

```
var sender chan<- int64        ①
var receiver <-chan float32     ②
```

① `sender` is a variable of type `chan<- int64`. `sender` is write-only.

② `receiver` is a variable of type `<-chan float32`. `receiver` is read-only.

9.10.1. Channel capacity

Although a channel is not technically a collection type, e.g., like an array, it behaves more or less like one. A FIFO queue, in particular. The size of a channel, or the size of the buffer in the channel, is called the "capacity".

A new channel value can be created using the built-in function `make`, which takes the `chan` type and capacity as its two arguments. For example,

```
ch := make(chan int, 100)
```

The newly created, and initialized, channel `ch` of type `chan int` has a capacity `100`. Up to 100 `int` values can be sent to this channel without retrieving any values from it. The channel will "block" when the number of items in the buffer reaches the channel's capacity, that is, when the channel is full.

When we "receive" a value from a non-empty channel, the value is removed from the channel. Channels indeed behave like a queue data structure.

One can also create an unbuffered channel, by specifying the `0` capacity, or by omitting the second argument in the `make` function call. For example,

```
unbuff := make(chan int)
```

For an unbuffered channel, like `unbuff` in this example, communication succeeds only when both a sender and receiver are ready to send a value and receive, respectively.

A channel can be closed with the built-in function `close`. Neither sender nor receiver can send/receive values on the closed channel.

9.11. Pointer Types

A pointer is an address to a variable (of a non-pointer type). The value of an uninitialized pointer is `nil`.

A pointer type denotes the set of all pointers to variables of a given type, called the base type of the pointer. For instance, for non-interface type T, *T is its pointer type. For *T, its base type is T.

Note that

- For a non-pointer type T, its base type is T itself.

- A base type cannot be a pointer or interface type.

Pointers provide reference semantics for the corresponding base type variables. For instance,

```
package main

func main() {
    i, j := 1, 2
    swap(&i, &j)
    println(i, j)
}

func swap(a, b *int) {
    *a, *b = *b, *a
}
```

This program will print out, *2, 1*.

9.12. Struct Types

A struct is a collection of a finite number of elements, called fields. Each field has a name and a type, and their order is significant in a struct.

Field names may be specified explicitly or implicitly (through embedding). Within a struct, non-blank field names must all be unique, regardless of their positions, and whether they are explicitly or implicitly named.

A struct type, named or otherwise, denotes a set of all structs that have the same field declarations, that is, the field names, their corresponding types, and their orders.

Syntactically, a struct type is defined by the keyword `struct`, followed by a sequence of fields, enclosed in angular braces ({ }). For instance,

```
var x struct { latitude, longitude float32 }
```

This declaration introduces the name `x`. The variable `x`'s type is an anonymous struct type with two fields, `latitude` and `longitude`, whose types are both `float32`.

```
type point2d struct { x, y int }
```

This type definition creates a new named struct type `point2d`. The `point2d` type and the anonymous type `struct { x, y int }` are two distinct types despite the fact that both denote structs comprising two `int` fields with the same names, `x` and `y`.

A struct with no fields is a valid struct:

```
type Huh struct {}          ①
```

① `Huh` is of the empty struct type.

It is idiomatic in Go to use a named empty struct type to "organize" (related) functions into a method set. This is further discussed later in the book, for example, in the Methods chapter.

9.12.1. Embedded Fields

A field declared with a type but no explicit field name is called an embedded field.

An embedded field must be specified as a type name T or as a pointer to a non-interface type *T, and T itself may not be a pointer type.

The unqualified type name acts as the field name.

9.12.2. Tags

A field declaration may be followed by an optional string literal tag, which becomes an attribute for all the fields in the corresponding field declaration.

For example,

```
type Point struct {
    X  float32  `json:"x"`
    Y  float32  `json:"y"`
}
```

9.12.3. Generic structs

There is no separate syntax for "generic structs". A named type with type parameters can be used to create a generic type with structs.

Chapter 10. Interfaces

10.1. Interface Types

An `interface` in Go defines a type, or more generally, a set of types (" type set").

- A variable of a basic interface type can be used for any type at run time (called the "dynamic type") that is in the type set of the declared interface (called the "static type").

- A general interface can be used to constrain a generic type parameter to the specified type set in the declarations of types and functions.

The zero value of an interface type is `nil`.

An interface type is specified by the keyword `interface`, followed by a list of zero, one, or more *interface elements*, enclosed in a pair of curly braces. Each interface element can be

- A method specification, e.g., a method name and signature,
- A (non-interface) type or underlying type, or
- A union (|) of two or more non-interface types or underlying types.

Syntactically, the underlying type of a non-interface type is indicated by the tilde symbol (~) in front of the type name. This syntax ~T can only be used with type T whose underlying type is T itself.

For example,

```
interface {
    ToFloat() float64        ①
}
```

```
interface {
    int                        ②
}

interface {
    ~int32                     ③
}

interface {
    bool | ~int8               ④
}
```

① An explicit method name and signature. This interface is a basic interface.

② This interface represents the int type.

③ This interface represents int32 and all other types whose underlying type is int32. Note that the underlying type of int32 is int32 itself.

④ The bool type or all types with the underlying type int8, including int8.

The type definition can be used to create named interface types, including generic interface types.

10.1.1. Embedded interface elements

An interface E may be embedded in another interface I. In that case, the type set of I includes all methods from the type set of E as well as those explicitly declared in I. Interface embedding can be nested.

For example,

```
type Animal interface {
    Eat()
    Sleep()
```

```
    }
```

```
type Man interface {
    Animal
    Laugh()
}
```

In this example, the interface type `Man` includes the following three methods, `Eat()`, `Sleep()`, and `Laugh()`. Since the names are not part of interfaces, this interface declaration, using the embedded interface syntax, is *equivalent* to the following:

```
interface {
    Eat()
    Sleep()
    Laugh()
}
```

10.2. Type Sets

The type set of an interface or non-interface type is determined as follows:

- The type set of the empty interface `interface{}` is the set of all non-interface types.

- The type set of a non-empty interface type is the *intersection* of all type sets of its interface elements.

- The type set of a method specification is the set of all types whose method sets include that method.

- The type set of a non-interface type is the set consisting of just that type.

- The type set of a term of the form ~T with a non-interface type T is the set of types whose underlying type is T.

- The type set of a union of two or more terms, t1 through tn, separated by | (e.g., t1 | t2 | … | tn) is the *union* of the type sets of those terms.

10.3. Implementing Interfaces

A value of a given type is said to "implement an interface" if the type implements the interface.

- A non-interface type T implements an interface I if it is an element of the type set of I.

- An interface type T implements an interface I if the type set of T is a subset of the type set of I.

For example,

```
type Drone struct {}
type Airplane struct {}

type Flyer interface {
    Fly()
}

type HighFlyer interface {
    Flyer
    FlyHigh() string
}

func (d Drone) Fly() {}
func (a Airplane) Fly() {}
func (a Airplane) FlyHigh() string {
    return "Yay!"
}
```

In this example, the type set of the interface `Flyer` is `Drone` and `Airplane` whereas the type sef of `HighFlyer` is `Airplane`. Therefore, a value of the `Drone` type implements `Flyer`, and a value of `Airplane` implements both `Flyer` and `HighFlyer`.

Furthermore, a value of the interface type `HighFlyer` implements `Flyer` since the `HighFlyer`'s type set is a subset of that of `Flyer`.

(Or, conversely, the method set of `Drone` is `Fly` whereas the method set of `Airplane` includes `Fly` and `FlyHigh`. Therefore, `Drone` implements `Flyer` and `Airplane` implements `Flyer` and `HighFlyer`.)

10.4. Basic Interfaces

An interface may contain only a list of one or more methods but nothing else. The type set defined by such an interface is the set of all types which implement all of those methods. An interface whose type set can be defined entirely by a list of methods is called the *basic interface*.

The "method set" of a basic interface type consists of the methods specified by that interface.

Only basic interface types can be used as the types of values or variables, or components of other non-interface types.

A type may implement several different interfaces, which may possibly overlap. Every type that implements a specific interface is a member of the type set of that interface. In particular, all types are a member of the type set of `any`, which is an alias name for the empty interface, `interface{}`.

For instance,

```
type Human struct {}
```

```
type Martian struct {}

type Player interface {
    Play()
}

type Drinker interface {
    Drink()
}

func (h Human) Play() {}
func (h Human) Drink() {}

func (m Martian) Drink() {}
```

In this example, the method set of `Human` is `Play()` and `Drink()`, and the method set of `Martian` is `Drink()`. Hence, the type set of `Player` is `Human`, and the type set of `Drinker` is `Human` and `Martian`.

Therefore, the type `Human` implements the `Player` and `Drinker` interfaces, and `Martian` implements `Drinker`. (And, both types automatically implement `interface{}`.)

10.5. General Interfaces

Since Go 1.18, the syntax of `interface` has been generalized. As we defined earlier, an interface declaration can now include non-interface type interface elements.

Furthermore, Go interfaces now correspond to type sets rather than to single (possibly polymorphic) types as it used to be the case with the basic interfaces prior to Go 1.18.

Interfaces, which are not basic interfaces, may only be used as generic type constraints, or as elements of other interfaces used as constraints.

Here's an example:

```
interface {
    ~int
    String() string
}
```

This interface represents all types with underlying type `int` which implement the `String` method. (This effectively excludes the builtin `int` type since it does not implement the `String` method.) This interface is not a basic interface, and it can only used in the context of generic type constraints.

 Go's generics, as currently designed, has some limitations. For example, there is no way to specify generic type constraints that includes `~string` types *or* any other types that implement the `String()` `string` method. In the previous example, the interface elements `~int` and `String()` `string` are combined as an intersection, not as a union.

Chapter 11. Functions

11.1. Function Types

- A *function signature* is the list of parameter types and the list of result types of a function.

- A function type denotes the set of all functions and methods with the same function signature.

- The value of an uninitialized variable of a function type is `nil`.

For example,

```
func (value int, flag bool) int          ①
```

① A function signature that takes `int` and `bool` parameters and returns an `int` value. Note that a function type/signature starts with the keyword `func`, and it is followed by a parameter list and then the return value types, if any.

```
func (lhs, rhs float32) (sum float32)     ①
```

① A function signature that takes two `float32` parameters and returns a `float32` value. The parameter and return value names are not part of a function signature/type. That is, this function signature is equivalent to `func (float32, float32) float32`.

11.1.1. Variadic functions

The type of the last input parameter in a function can be prefixed with a token .... A function with such a parameter is called variadic, and it may be invoked with zero or more arguments for that parameter.

For example,

```
func Sum(numbers ...int) int {          ①
    /* ... */
}
```

① The function type of this function is `func (...int) int`.

This `Sum` function can be called with zero, one, or more `int` values.

```
s1 := Sum()
s2 := Sum(10)
s3 := Sum(1, 2, 3)
// ...
```

11.2. Function Declarations

The set of top-level declarations in Go includes function and method declarations.

A function is essentially a function signature plus a function body (implementation). *A function declaration* binds an identifier, i.e., a function name, to a function. A function body is syntactically a block. For example,

```
func First(fst, snd int) int          ①
{                                      ②
    return fst
}
```

① The `func` keyword, function name (`First`), and the function signature.

② The function body block (from { to }).

If the function's signature declares result parameters, the function body's statement list must end with a terminating statement.

```
func FindSubstring(str, sub string) int {
    // Statement list, possibly including return statements.

    // If sub is not found in str, just return -1.
    return -1                    ①
}
```

① The final terminating statement is required.

11.3. Generic Functions

If the function declaration specifies type parameters, the function name denotes a *generic function*. Generic functions define a set of functions (or, function templates) parametrized by types, and they must be *instantiated* when they are used.

The type parameters of a function appear between brackets, before the function's arguments. Generic type constraints are required for all type parameters.

```
func min[T constraints.Ordered](x, y T) T     ①
{
    if x < y {                                 ②
        return x
    }
    return y
}
```

① The type parameter T is constrained by the Ordered interface.

② Only the values of x and y in the type set of Ordered can be used for comparison in this conditional expression.

The `min` function can be used as follows, for instance:

```
m := min[int](1, 10)
```

In this particular example, the arguments are untyped integer literals, and hence the type argument can be omitted, e.g., as in `min(1, 10)`. T will be presumed to be `int`. The type of `m` will be `int` as well (since `min` returns a value of type `T`). This is known as the type parameter inference.

11.4. Function Literals

A function literal represents an anonymous function.

```
func(a, b int, z float64) bool { return a*b < int(z) }   ①
```

① Note that an anonymous function has no function name.

A function literal can be either directly invoked, or it can be assigned to a variable, which can be invoked later.

```
f := func(x, y int) int { return x + y }        ①
sum := f(1, 2)                                   ②
func(ch chan int) { ch <- ACK }(replyChan)       ③
```

① An anonymous function is assigned to a variable `f`.

② `f` is callable.

③ An anonymous function can also be called directly.

Function literals are closures. They may refer to variables defined in a surrounding function.

Those "closed-over variables" are then shared between the surrounding function and the function literal, and they survive as long as they are accessible (e.g., even after the stack frame of the surrounding function is deleted).

Here's an example code to generate Fibonacci sequence, using an anonymous function.

```go
package main

import (
    "fmt"
)

func fib() func() int {                 ①
    a, b := 0, 1

    return func() int {                 ②
        a, b = b, a+b                   ③
        return a
    }
}

func main() {
    f := fib()

    for x := f(); x < 100; x = f() {
        fmt.Println(x)
    }
}
```

① The `fib` function returns a function of type `func() int`.

② The `fib` function returns an anonymous function, which is a closure.

③ Note that the variables `a` and `b` are declared in the enclosing function.

Chapter 12. Methods

12.1. Method Declarations

A method is a function with a *receiver*.

A method declaration binds an identifier, a method name, to a method, and associates the method with *the receiver's base type*.

Here's the method declaration syntax:

```
func ( ReceiverParameter ) MethodName ( ParameterList ) Result
FunctionBodyBlock
```

ReceiverParameter should be one of the following two forms,

- `name T`, or
- `name *T`,

for a non-pointer, non-interface type `T`. The name can be a blank identifier (`_`), or it can be entirely omitted, if the receiver's value is not referenced inside the body of the method.

The rest of the method syntax is more or less identical to that of function declarations. For example,

```
type Pt1D float32

func (p Pt1D) Dist() float32 {        ①
    if p >= 0 {
        return p
    }
    return -p
```

```
    }
```

① The method `Dist` is defined for the receiver p with type `Pt1D`, whose base type is `Pt1D`.

A method declaration itself cannot introduce type parameters like a function declaration, however. If the receiver base type is a generic type, the receiver parameter must include the corresponding type parameters, but not the type parameter constraint. The receiver type constraint is *implied* by the receiver's base type definition.

For example,

```
type MapElement[K comparable, V any] struct {
    key    K                              ①
    value  V
}

func (e MapElement[K, V]) Key() K {       ②
    return e.key
}

func (e MapElement[T, S]) Value() S {     ③
    return e.value
}
```

① The fields `key` and `value` are not exported, in this example, while the type itself is exported.

② The type parameters, K and V, are associated with the receiver e. The type parameter K is constrained to `comparable` although it is not explicitly specified here. Note that the `Key` method provides a readonly access to the field `key` (e.g., from outside the package).

③ Just for illustration, we use different symbols for the type parameters. The type constraints of T and S are the same, that is, `comparable` and `any`, respectively.

One important thing to note is that methods must be defined in the same package as the base type of the receiver. That is, among other things, you cannot define methods for the types that you do not "own", including all builtin types.

A method declaration binds the method to its receiver base type. The method name is visible only within the selectors for receiver type T, or *T, and for its base type T.

(Note that when the receiver's type is T (a non-pointer, non-interface type), the method is available only for T. On the other hand, when the receiver's type is *T, the method is available for both T and *T.)

It is a common practice in Go to use a type as sort of a namespace to organize (related) functions, for example, as alluded earlier in the context of empty struct types.

Using the same example,

```
type Huh struct {}            ①

func (_ Huh) M1() {}          ②
func (*Huh) M2() {}           ③

var h Huh                     ④
h.M1()                        ⑤
h.M2()                        ⑥
```

① An empty struct type, e.g., with no fields.

② The name of a receiver is not needed when we do not use it.

③ Likewise.

④ The variable h is of the type Huh.

⑤ M1 is available only as a method of a variable of type Huh. M2 is available only as a method of a variable of type Huh or *Huh.

⑥ Note that h.M1() and h.M2(), using the method call syntax, are more or less equivalent to Huh.M1(h) and Huh.M2(h), respectively, using the function call syntax.

A function signature of a method is that of a function with the receiver as its first parameter. For instance, for the following method,

```
func (ship *Ship) Move(speed float32) bool {
    // ...
}
```

The signature of the method Move is

```
func (ship *Ship, speed float32) bool
```

Note that there is no such a thing as a method literal in Go. One can always use an anonymous function with a receiver as its first argument.

Chapter 13. Expressions

An expression computes, and returns a value, by applying functions or other operators to its operands.

13.1. Operands

Operands denote the elementary values in an expression. An operand may be

- A literal,
- A non-blank identifier denoting
    ◦ a constant,
    ◦ variable, or
    ◦ function, or
- A parenthesized expression.

An operand name denoting a generic function may be followed by a list of type arguments. The resulting operand is an instantiated function.

13.2. Addressable Expressions

The following expressions are deemed "addressable":

- A variable,
- Pointer indirection,
- Slice indexing operation,
- A field selector of an addressable struct operand, or
- An array indexing operation of an addressable array.

13.3. Primary Expressions

Primary expressions are the simplest expressions that can be used as operands of unary and binary operators.

The following are syntactically primary expressions:

- Type conversion expressions,

- <<[part02-chapter-methods, Method expressions>>, and

- Primary expressions followed by

    ◦ Selector,

    ◦ Index,

    ◦ Slice,

    ◦ Type assertion, **or**

    ◦ Function argument.

13.4. Constant Expressions

Constant expressions are evaluated at compile time, and they can only contain constant operands.

Constants can be *untyped*:

- Untyped Boolean constants can be used where boolean values can be used.

- Untyped numeric constants can be used where integer or floating-point values can be used.

- Untyped string constants can be used in places where strings can be used.

A constant comparison always yields an untyped boolean constant. Any other operation on untyped constants results in an untyped constant of the same kind.

Constant expressions are evaluated *exactly*. Untyped numerical constants are infinite precision in Go, only limited by practical constraints.

13.4.1. Conversions

A constant value x can be converted to type T if x is representable by a value of T. Converting an untyped constant yields a typed constant as a result.

```
x := uint(10)                    ①
y := float32(-1e-100)            ②
```

① The RHS expression is a constant 10 of the uint type, and hence x is of type uint.

② The RHS expression is a constant 0.0 of type float32, and hence y is float32 as well.

13.5. Composite Literals

Composite literals are used to construct new values for arrays, slices, maps, and structs.

Each type of literal consists of the relevant type name followed by a list of elements of the given type enclosed in a pair of matching curly braces ({}).

```
[3]int{1, 10, 100}               ①
[]bool{true, false}              ②
```

① An array literal that creates a 3 element array, with elements, 1, 10, and 100. The number of elements need not be explicitly specified.

For example, this literal syntax is equivalent to `[…]int{1, 10, 100}`.

② A slice literal that creates a 2 element slice, with elements, `true` and `false`. Note that the empty pair of square brackets is used to denote a slice.

```
var x = map[string]int{}                    ①
```

① The map literal creates an empty map of type `map[string]int`. This map value is assigned to the variable `x` through assignment.

```
type Location struct {
    Lat, Lon float64
}

var loc = Location{37.7, -122.4}       ①
```

① The expression on the RHS of the assignment statement is a struct literal that constructs a new Location value with `Lat = 37.7` and `Lon = -122.4`.

Each element may be preceded by a corresponding key. The key is interpreted as

- A field name for struct literals,
- An index for array and slice literals, and
- A key for map literals.

For example,

```
[...]float32{0: 0.1, 1: 0.2}                    ①
```

① An array literal with two elements. This literal is equivalent to

```
[2]float32{0.1, 0.2}.
```

```
type Coordinate struct {
    X, Y uint
}

var position = Coordinate{X: 0, Y: 10}      ①
```

① The RHS struct literal is the same as `Coordinate{0, 10}` or `Coordinate{Y: 10, X: 0}`. When the field names are specified, the order is not significant.

For map literals, all elements must have keys.

```
var pop = map[string]float32{             ①
    "New York City": 8.5,
    "Los Angeles": 4.0,
}
```

① The right-hand side map literal creates a new mapof two elements of type `map[string]float32`. This map value is assigned to the variable `pop` through assignment. The type of `pop` is `map[string]float32`.

13.6. Index Expressions

An index expression, `a[i]`, is used to denote an element of `a` of type

- Array,
- Pointer to array,
- Slice,
- String, or
- Map.

13.6. Index Expressions

The value i is called the *key* in case of maps, or the *index* otherwise.

```
fibonacci := [8]int{0, 1, 1, 2, 3, 5, 7, 13}        ①
fibslice := fibonacci[:]                             ②
ptrfib := &fibonacci                                 ③

a := fibonacci[3]                                    ④
b := fibslice[4]                                     ⑤
c := ptrfib[5]                                       ⑥

fibonacci[6] = 8                                     ⑦
```

① `fibonacci` is an array of type `[8]int`. This includes the first 8 elements of (somewhat incorrect) Fibonacci sequence.

② `fibslice` is a slice of type `[]int`.

③ `ptrfib` is a pointer to the array `fibonacci`, whose type is `[8]int`.

④ The type and value of a are `int` and 2, respectively.

⑤ The type and value of b are `int` and 3, respectively.

⑥ The type and value of c are `int` and 5, respectively. Note that the index expression `ptrfib[5]` is equivalent to `(*ptrfib)[5]`.

⑦ After this assignment, the values of `fibonacci[6]`, `fibslice[6]`, and `*ptrfib[6]` are all 8 (the correct Fibonacci number).

In case of map indexing, Go provides a special form when an index expression is used in initialization or assignment. For instance, for a map m of type `map[K]V`, and for a key k of type K, `m[k]` returns two values.

For example,

```
v, ok := m[k]
```

The first value v is the usual value of an index expression, of type V. The second value ok is an untyped boolean constant. The value of ok is true if the key x is present in the map, and false otherwise.

When the first return value is not needed, the blank identifier (_) can be used. When the second boolean return value is not needed, the blank identifier (_) can be used likewise, or it can be omitted.

For instance,

```
_, ok := m[k]          ①
v := m[k]              ②
```

① Depending on whether m contains an element with key k, that is, depending on the value of ok, we can do further processing.

② When we are sure that m contains an element with key k, we can ignore the second return value. This statement is equivalent to v, _ := m[k].

13.7. Slice Expressions

Slice expressions construct a substring or slice from a string, array, pointer to array, or slice.

13.7.1. Substrings

For a string s, the following slicing operation creates a substring, from index low (inclusive) to high (exclusive).

```
s[low : high]
```

Either low or high, or both, can be omitted. The default values are 0 and len(s), for low and high, respectively.

For example,

```
str := "hello, world!"
sub := str[:4]                    ①
```

① sub is a string `"hell"`.

13.7.2. Slices

For an array, pointer to array, or slice, there are two variants of slice expressions.

As with the string slice expressions, a slice of an array, a pointer to array, or another slice, can be taken by specifying a range, from index `low` (inclusive) to `high` (exclusive). For example, the following expression returns a slice of a with the specified range:

```
a[low : high]
```

The new slice has indices starting at 0 and length equal to `high` - `low`. If the `low` and/or `high` values are omitted, then their default values are used, 0 for `low` and `len(a)` for `high`. For example, a[:] is equivalent to a[0 : len(a)].

```
a := []int{1, 2, 3, 4, 5}      ①
s := a[1:4]                     ②
```

① The RHS expression is a slice literal of type [ ]int with 5 elements.

② The RHS is a slice expression, which returns a slice of type [ ]int with 3 elements. It includes 3 elements, 2, 3, 4.

In addition, slicing can also be done using the following syntax:

```
a[low : high : max]
```

This expression constructs a slice of the same type, and with the same length and elements as the simple slice expression a[low : high]. Additionally, it controls the new slice's capacity by setting it to max - low. In this syntax, only the first index may be omitted, whose default value is 0.

```
a := [5]int{1, 2, 3, 4, 5}
t := a[1:3:5]                                    ①
```

① t refers to a slice of type []int with length 2 (3 - 1) and capacity 4 (5 - 1).

13.8. Selectors

For a primary expression x that is not a package name, the selector expression x.f denotes the field or method f of the value x. If x is a package name, then the dot notation refers to qualified identifiers.

The identifier f is called the field selector or method selector depending on whether f is a field or method, respectively. The type of the selector expression is that of f.

For example,

```
type Point struct {
    X, Y float32
}

func (p *Point) Move(dx, dy float32) {
    p.X += dx                                    ①
    p.Y += dy
}
```

```
func (p *Point) MoveHorz(distance float32) {
  p.Move(distance, 0.0)                              ②
}
```

① The field X of the value p is accessed via the field selector expression, p.X. The type of p.X is float32, the same as X. Note that the type of p is *Point, and p.X is equivalent to (*p).X.

② The method Move on the value p is called, in this example, using the method selector expression, p.Move(distance, 0.0), which is equivalent to (*p).Move(distance, 0.0) since p is a pointer type.

13.9. Function and Method Calls

Given an expression f of function type F, the following expression calls f with arguments a1, a2, ... an.

```
f(a1, a2, /* ... */ an)
```

Each argument must be a single-valued expression assignable to the corresponding parameter type of F. All arguments are evaluated before the function is called. The type of the call expression is the result type of F.

A method invocation is similar but the method itself is specified as a selector upon a value of the receiver type for the method.

```
math.Cos(x, y)              ①
var pt *Point
pt.Move(3.5, 5.5)           ②
```

① A function call.

② A method call with receiver pt.

In a function call,

- The function value and arguments are evaluated in the usual order first,

- After they are evaluated, the parameters of the call are *passed by value* to the function,

- Then the called function begins execution, and

- The return parameters of the function are *passed by value* back to the calling function when the function execution ends.

13.9.1. Passing arguments to ... parameters

The final parameter of a function f can be specified as p ...T, for a parameter name p and a type T. In such as case, the type of p is equivalent to type [ ]T within the body of f.

First, if the function f is invoked with no actual arguments for p, then the value passed to p is nil.

Otherwise, the value passed is a new slice of type [ ]T with a new underlying array with the successive arguments as its elements. The length, and the capacity, of the slice in a particular call is therefore the number of arguments bound to p in the call.

As an example, given a function,

```
func SendMoney(amount float32, names ...string)
```

The values of names in the calls SendMoney(100.0) and SendMoney(100.0, "Joe", "Jill") are nil and [ ]string{"Joe", "Jill"}, respectively.

13.10. Conversions

A conversion expression changes the type of a given expression to the type specified by the conversion. A conversion may be implicitly done by the context in which an expression appears. Or, a conversion may be explicitly specified.

An explicit conversion is an expression of the form T(x) where T is a type and x is an expression that can be converted to type T.

Conversion of constant values is explained in Constant expression conversions.

A non-constant value x can be converted to type T if any of the following holds:

- x is assignable to T,
- x's type and T have identical underlying types,
- x's type and T are pointer types that are not defined types, and their pointer base types have identical underlying types,
- x's type and T are both integer or floating point types,
- x's type and T are both complex number types,
- x is an integer or a slice of bytes or runes and T is a string type, or
- x is a string and T is a slice of bytes or runes.

Struct tags are ignored when comparing struct types for identity for the purposes of conversion.

13.11. Type Assertions

A type assertion x.(T) takes an expression x of an interface type (e.g., a static type) and a target type T (e.g., a dynamic type), and it asserts that

- x is not `nil`, and

- The value stored in x is of type T.

If the assertion holds, then it return the value stored in x as type T. Otherwise, a runtime panic occurs.

13.11.1. Type assertions in assignments

A type assertion used in an assignment or initialization returns an additional untyped boolean value, as its second return value. For example,

```
v, ok := x.(T)
```

When the assertion succeeds, the value of `ok` is `true`. When the assertion fails, no run-time panic occurs in this form of type assertions. Instead, the value of `ok` is set to `false` and the value of v is set to the zero value for type T.

Either return value can be ignored using the blank identifier (_). When the second return value is not needed, e.g., because we know that the type assertion will always succeed, it can be entirely omitted. For instance, the following is a valid syntax.

```
v := x.(T)
```

13.12. Operators

Operators combine operands into expressions.

Binary operators combine two expressions into one. Unary operators take a single operand expression, and convert it into another expression that can be used with either unary or binary operators.

Binary operators in Go can be classified into four groups.

13.12.1. Logical operators

```
|| &&
```

13.12.2. Relational operators

```
== != < <= > >=
```

13.12.3. Additive operators

```
+ - | ^
```

13.12.4. Multiplicative operators

```
* / % << >> & &^
```

13.12.5. Unary operators

In addition, the following can be used as unary operators:

```
+ - ! ^ * & <-
```

13.12.6. Operator precedence

Unary operators have the highest precedence.

There are five precedence levels for binary operators. Multiplication operators bind the strongest, followed by addition operators, comparison operators, && (logical AND), and finally || (logical OR):

```
Precedence     Operator
5              *  /  %  <<  >>  &  &^
4              +  -  |  ^
3              ==  !=  <  <=  >  >=
2              &&
1              ||
```

Binary operators of the same precedence associate from left to right. For instance, x / y * z is the same as (x / y) * z.

Since the increment (++) and decrement (--) operators form statements, they are not part of expressions and they are not considered for the purposes of operator precedence. Therefore, for example, a statement p++ is the same as (p)++ where p is an expression.

13.13. Arithmetic Operators

Arithmetic operators take two numeric values, and they return a result of the same type as the first operand.

The four standard arithmetic operators (+, -, *, /) are used with operands of integer, floating-point, and complex types.

+   Sum

−   Difference

*   Product

/   Quotient

%   Remainder

The bitwise logical and shift operators can be used with integers only.

&   Bitwise AND

| Bitwise OR

^   Bitwise XOR

&^   Bit clear (AND NOT)

<<   Left shift

>>   Right shift

13.13.1. String concatenation

Strings can be concatenated using the + operator, or using the +=
assignment statement. String addition creates a new string by
concatenating the two operands.

```
s := "hello " + "world"        ①
s += " and you"                ②
```

① The value of s is "hello world".

② The value of s is now "hello world and you".

13.14. Comparison operators

A binary comparison operator takes two operands, compares their
values, and returns an untyped boolean value as a result. One operand
must be assignable to the type of the other operand.

==   Equal to

!=   Not equal to

<   Less than

<=   Less than or equal to

>   Greater than

>=   Greater than or equal to

The equality operators == and != apply to operands that are *comparable.* The ordering operators <, <=, >, and >= apply to operands that are *ordered.*

The values of slice, map, and function types are not generally comparable except when they are compared to nil. Comparison of pointer, channel, and interface values to nil is also allowed.

13.15. Logical Operators

Logical operators take boolean values as arguments and they return a result of the same type as the arguments.

&&   Binary conditional AND

|| Binary conditional OR

!   Unary NOT

For the unary logical expression !p, its value is true if p == false. Otherwise, it is false.

The right operand of a binary logical operator is evaluated conditionally. This is known as the "short circuiting".

In case of p && q, q is evaluated only if p evaluates to true.

- It returns `false` if p `==` `false`.

- Otherwise it returns the value of the second expression q.

In case of p `||` q, q is evaluated only if p evaluates to `false`.

- It return `true` if p `==` `true`.

- Otherwise, it returns the value of q.

13.16. Address Operators

For an operand x of type T, the address operation &x generates a pointer to x, whose type is *T.

The operand of the address operator & must be addressable. Or, the operand may also be a (possibly parenthesized) composite literal expression.

If the evaluation of x would cause a run-time panic, then so does the evaluation of &x.

13.17. Receive Operator

A unary receive operator (<-) takes an operand ch of type chan T and it returns the value received from the channel ch. The type of the r eceive operation (<-ch) is the element type of the channel (T).

The channel direction must be compatible with the receive operations.

The receive expression blocks until a value is available. Receiving from a nil channel blocks forever.

```
v1 := <-ch
f(<-ch)
```

```
<-ch                    ①
```

① It wait until it receives a value and it discards the received value.

13.17.1. Receive operator in assignments

A receive expression used in an assignment or initialization returns an additional untyped boolean result as its second value to indicate whether the receive operation succeeded.

```
v, ok := <-ch
```

The value of `ok` is `true` if the value received was delivered by a successful send operation to the channel. It is `false` otherwise, for example, because the channel is closed and empty.

The second return value can be ignored. For instance, the following is a syntactically valid statement:

```
v := <-ch
```

Chapter 14. Statements

Statements control execution of a program. There are roughly 20 different kinds of statements in Go. The following are classified as *simple statements*:

- Empty statements,
- Short variable declarations,
- Assignments,
- Increment/Decrement statements,
- Expression statements, and
- Send statements.

There are 13 more different statements:

- Declarations,
- Labeled statements,
- If statements,
- For statements,
- Switch statements,
- Select statements,
- Fallthrough statements,
- Continue statements,
- Break statements,
- Goto statements,
- Defer statements,
- Return statements, and
- Go statements.

In addition, a block is syntactically a statement. That is, a block can be used where a statement is expected.

14.1. Empty statements

The empty statement does nothing.

```
package main

func main() {
    ;                       ①
    ;;                      ②
}
```

① Normally, we do not use semicolons when writing Go programs. The semicolon here is included for illustration since one cannot see an empty statement.

② This line includes two empty statements.

14.2. Assignments

An assignment is a simple statement that binds each operand from a *list of expressions*, on the left hand side of an assignment operator, to the corresponding value in another *list of expressions* on the right hand side.

There are two kinds of assignment statements. Here's an example of a simple assignment using the assignment operator =:

```
package main

import "fmt"

func main() {
```

```
    var apple, orange string              ①
    apple, orange = "sweet", "sour"       ②
    fmt.println(apple, orange)            ③
}
```

① A variable declaration. Not an assignment.

② A simple assignment statement, using the assignment operator =.

③ This will print out "sweet sour".

In this type of an assignment, expressions on the RHS are evaluated first, from left to right, *before* their values are assigned to the corresponding expressions on the LHS.

The following are also assignment operators in Go (each treated as a *single token*):

```
+=  -=  |=  ^=  *=  /=  %=  <<=  >>=  &=  &^=
```

An assignment statement of this form x op= y, where op= schematically represents an assignment operator listed above, is more or less equivalent to x = x op (y). But, in x op= y, x is evaluated only once.

In this kind of assignment operations,

- Each expression list on both sides can contain only one expression,

- The left-hand expression cannot be the blank identifier (_), and

- The left-hand expression is evaluated first before the right-hand expression.

```
package main

func main() {
```

```
    var myFortune, expense = 1000, 999      ①
    myFortune -= expense                     ②
    fmt.printf("My remaining fortune is %d dollars.\n",
myFortune)
}
```

① Variable declaration with initialization.

② An assignment statement of the second kind. This statement is equivalent to `myFortune = myFortune - expense`.

14.2.1. The left-hand side operand

In general, each left-hand side operand in an assignment that is not the blank identifier must be

- Addressable, or

- A map index expression.

```
x := 3
a[x] = "hey"
```

14.3. Increment - Decrement Statements

In Go, `++` and `--` are not operators unlike in many other C-style programming languages.

Instead, Go provides the *increment (++) and decrement (--) statements,* which can be used to increment and decrement their numeric operands by the untyped numeric constant 1, respectively.

An increment statement comprises an expression followed by `++`. Likewise, a decrement statement is an expression followed by `--`.

```
package main

func main() {
    i, j := 0, 0

    i++                 ①
    j--                 ②

    println(i, j)
}
```

① An increment statement.

② A decrement statement.

This program is semantically equivalent to the following:

```
package main

func main() {
    i, j := 0, 0

    i += 1
    j -= 1

    println(i, j)
}
```

As with the left-hand expression in the assignment statements, the operand expression of the increment or decrement statement must be

- Addressable, or

- A map index expression.

14.4. Expression Statements

The following expressions can be appear in statement context, and their values are ignored:

- Function calls (with the exception of a few builtin functions),
- Method calls, and
- Receive operations.

For example,

```
h(x+y)          ①
f.Close()       ②
(<-ch)          ③
```

① h is function.

② Close is a method defined on f.

③ A receive operation <-ch is used as a statement. Note that expression statements can be (optionally) parenthesized.

14.5. Send Statements

A send statement (channel <- expression) sends a value on a given channel:

- The left-hand channel expression must be of the chan type,
- The channel direction must permit send operations (e.g., chan T or chan<- T), and
- The value of the right-hand expression must be assignable to the channel's element type, T.

For example,

```
package main

func main() {
    ch1 := make(chan<- int, 10)
    ch2 := make(chan int)

    ch1 <- 3                        ①
    ch2 <- 2 + 5                    ②
}
```

① Send a value 3 to channel `ch1`.

② Send a value 7 (`2 + 5`) to channel `ch2`.

14.6. If Statements

The `if` statement is a compound statement, and it comprises

- The `if` keyword,

- A conditional/Boolean expression, followed by

- A block.

If the Boolean expression evaluates to `true`, then the statements in the `if` block is executed.

The `if` clause can be optionally followed by

- The keyword `else`, and

  ∘ Another block of statements, or

  ∘ Another `if` statement with its own optional `else` clause, and so forth.

If the conditional expression evaluates to `false`, then the statements in the `else` block is executed, if present.

The Boolean expression can be optionally preceded by a simple statement. This statement, if present, executes before the expression is evaluated.

```
package main

func main() {
    x := 0
    if x <= 10 {                            ①
        println("x is small")
    } else if max := 100; x > max {         ②
        println("x is big")
    } else {                                ③
        println("x is perfect")
    }
}
```

① An `if` statement.

② Another `if` statement in the `else` clause, which is part of the first/outer `if` statement. The conditional expression `x > max` in the second/inner `if` statement is preceded by a simple statement, `max := 100` followed by a semicolon `;`, in this example.

③ Syntactically, the `else` clause in this line belongs to the second `if` statement.

14.7. Labeled statements

A labeled statement is a composite statement. It is syntactically a combination of

- A label,
- A colon (`:`), followed by
- Another statement.

Any valid identifier can be used as a label.

```
package main

func main() {
    i := 0

begin:                          ①
    if i = i + 1; i < 10 {
        goto begin
    }
}
```

① The label `begin`, `:`, and the `if` statement form a single labeled statement.

A labeled statement can be used as a target of a `goto`, `break` or `continue` statement in the same scope. It is illegal to have unused labels in a block.

14.8. For Statements

A `for` statement is used for repeated execution of a block of statements.

The `for` statements can be classified into four different categories based on how the iteration is controlled.

- First, the iteration condition may not be explicitly specified.
- Otherwise, the iteration can be specified by
    - A single conditional expression,
    - A "for clause", or
    - A "range clause".

14.8.1. Infinite `for` loops

```
for { /* ... */ }
```

In its simplest form, the `for` statement repeats execution of the given block indefinitely. For example,

```
package main

func main() {
    for {
        println("I didn't do it.")        ①
    }
}
```

① A reference to Bart Simpson. ☺

This program will repeatedly print out *I didn't do it.* until it is terminated (in some way).

14.8.2. **For statements with single condition**

```
for Expression { /* ... */ }
```

In this form, the *Expression* must be a Boolean condition. The `for` statement executes the block repeatedly as long as the *Expression* evaluates to `true`. The condition is re-evaluated *before each iteration.*

```
package main

func main() {
    i, sum := 0, 0
    for i < 10 {                          ①
```

```
        sum += i
        i++
    }
    println("sum =", sum)          ②
}
```

① This use of `for` is similar to `while` found in other C-style languages.

② This program will print out *sum = 45*.

14.8.3. For statements with `for` clause

The "for clause" consists of three parts.

```
for SimpleStatement ; Expression ; SimpleStatement { /* ... */
}
```

The simple statements before the first semicolon and after the second semicolon are optional. The two semicolons are required in this syntactic form of `for` statements.

The `Expression` in the middle must evaluate to a Boolean value. The `for` clause `for` statement is controlled by this Boolean condition.

- The first simple statement, if any, is executed once *before the first iteration.*

- The Boolean expression is evaluated *before each iteration.*

- The last simple statement, if present, is executed *after each iteration.*

```
package main

func main() {
    sum := 0
    for i := 0; i < 10; i++ {          ①
        sum += i
```

```
    }
    println("sum =", sum)
}
```

① This is a classic C-style `for` loop.

14.8.4. `For` statements with `range` clause

The *range clause* `for` statement can be used to iterate through all entries in a `range` expression. It can be an iterable type of array, slice, map, or string. Or, it can be a channel permitting receive operations.

For each entry, it executes the block, after assigning the iteration values to the corresponding iteration variables, if specified.

There are three distinct forms:

```
for range Expression { /* ... */ }
```

```
for ExpressionList = range Expression { /* ... */ }
```

The iteration values are assigned to the respective iteration variables as in an assignment statement.

```
for IdentifierList := range Expression { /* ... */ }
```

In this form, the short variable declaration syntax is used. The variables' types are set to the types of the respective iteration values. Their scope is the block of the `for` statement.

For example,

```
package main

func main() {
    arr := []int{1, 3, 5}

    length := 0
    for range arr {                      ①
        length++
    }
    println("length =", length)

    e, sum := 0, 0
    for _, e = range arr {               ②
        sum += e
    }
    println("sum =", sum)

    idx, max := -1, 0
    for i, e := range arr {              ③
        if max < e {
            idx, max = i, e
        }
    }
    if idx >= 0 {
        println("idx =", idx, "max =", max)
    }
}
```

① We ignore the values of the elements.

② We ignore the index of each element in this example.

③ The variables i and e are reused in each iteration.

14.9. Switch Statements

A switch statement includes one or more branches of execution, called cases, based on the switch expression.

```
switch Expression { /* case clauses */ }
```

The *Expression* can be optionally preceded by a simple statement:

```
switch SimpleStatement ; Expression { /* case clauses */ }
```

There are two forms of `switch` statements, expression switches and type switches.

Expression switch

The cases contain expressions that are compared against the value of the `switch` expression.

Type switch

The cases contain types that are compared against the type of a specially annotated `switch` expression.

14.9.1. Expression switches

In an expression `switch` statement,

- The switch expression is first evaluated, and
- The case expressions are evaluated in order, from top to bottom:
  - The first one that equals the switch expression, if present, triggers execution of the statements of the associated case, and all the remaining cases are skipped.
  - Otherwise, if no case matches, then
    - If there is a *default* case, its statements are executed, and
    - If not, no statements are executed.

The `case` clause has the following syntax:

```
case ExpressionList : StatementList
```

An expression switch statement can have at most one `default` case clause:

```
default : StatementList
```

The last non-empty statement of the `StatementList` of a non-last case clause may be a `fallthrough statement`, in which case control should "fall through" to the next case clause.

Here are a few examples of the expression `switch` statement.

```
var result string

switch num {
default: result = "Don't know"      ①
case 1, 3, 5: result = "Odd"
case 2, 4, 6: result = "Even"
}
```

① The `default` case is always checked last regardless where it is placed. That is, for example, if `num` is `4`, then `result` becomes `"Even"` at the end of this `switch` statement.

```
switch {                            ①
case x < 0: return -x
case x >= 0: return x
}
```

① A missing switch expression is equivalent to `true`. That is, `switch { … }` is the same as `switch true { … }`.

```
switch x := f(); x - 10 {              ①
case 0: return "10"
default: return "Not 10"
}
```

① A simple statement, a short variable declaration x := f() in this example, can precede the switch expression, x - 10 in this case.

14.9.2. Type switches

A type switch statement compares types rather than values. It is marked by a special switch expression, expression.(type):

```
switch x.(type) { /* case clauses */ }
```

Or, alternatively,

```
switch y := x.(type) { /* case clauses */ }
```

In this form, the variable y is bound to the asserted type (which could be nil).

As with the expression switch statement, the type switch expression (either form) can also be preceded by a simple statement (and a semicolon), which is executed before the type switch expression is evaluated.

The case clause has the following syntax:

```
case TypeList : StatementList
```

where *TypeList* is a comma-separated list of one or more types.

In this form, cases are compared with dynamic or runtime type of the expression x. As in type assertions, x must be of an interface type, and each non-interface type T listed in a case must implement the type of x.

For example,

```go
switch x := f(); t := x.(type) {
case int:
    fmt.Printf("Int x = %d\n", x)
case float64:
    fmt.Printf("Float64 x = %f\n", x)
case func(int) int:
    fmt.Println("x is a function of type 'func(int) int'")
default:
    fmt.Printf("The type of x is %v\n", t)
}
```

14.10. Select Statements

A select statement branches on a set of one or more (send or receive) channel operations. It is similar to the switch statement, but, in the select statement, all cases refer to communication operations.

```go
select { /* communication clauses */ }
```

The communication case clause has the following syntax:

```go
case SendStatement : StatementList
```

Or,

```go
case ReceiveStatement : StatementList
```

The *SendStatement* is one of the compound statement types in Go, send statement, e.g., ch<- v. The *ReceiveStatement* can be in one of the following three forms:

- A receive operation used by itself as an expression statement, e.g., <-ch.

- A receive operation used in an assignment statement, e.g., arr[2] = <-ch.

- A receive operation used in a short variable declaration statement, e.g., x := <-ch.

Similar to switch statements, the select statement can also have an optional default case:

```
default : StatementList
```

Here's a simple example use of the select statement:

```
package main

import "fmt"

func lucasSequence(ch chan int, done chan bool) {
    a, b := 2, 1                              ①

    for {
        select {                              ②
        case ch <- a:                         ③
            a, b = b, a+b                      ④
        case <-done:                          ⑤
            return
        }
    }
}
```

```go
func main() {
    ch := make(chan int)
    done := make(chan bool)

    go func() {
        for i := 1; i <= 10; i++ {
            fmt.Println(i, "->", <-ch)
        }
        done <- true
    }()

    lucasSequence(ch, done)
}
```

① Lucas numbers are generated in the same way Fibonacci numbers are generated. The only difference is that the first two numbers are 2 and 1 instead of 1 and 1 of the Fibonacci sequence.

② Note the use of the `select` statement in an infinite `for` loop.

③ A `case` clause with *SendStatement*.

④ The n-th Lucas/Fibonacci number is the sum of ($n-1$)-th and ($n-2$) -th numbers.

⑤ A `case` clause with *ReceiveStatement*.

Note the idiomatic use of channels and go routines in this example. Most modern programming languages have constructs like generators and coroutines, etc. (e.g., the `yield` statement). Go doesn't. Go instead uses channels to accomplish the similar tasks, among other things. In this example, `lucasSequence`, for instance, can be viewed as a generator function.

14.11. Fallthrough Statements

A `fallthrough` statement transfers control to the first statement of the next `case` (or, `default`) clause in the expression switch statements. The `fallthrough` statement is not permitted in the type switch statements.

In the following example, when x is greater than 100, it prints out three lines, which are all true statements. When x is greater than 10 but less than or equal to 100, it prints out two lines. When x is between 1 and 10, it prints out one line, *I'm positive.*

```
switch {
case x > 100:
  fmt.Println("I'm bigger than 100")
  fallthrough
case x > 10:
  fmt.Println("I'm bigger than 10")
  fallthrough
case x > 0:
  fmt.Println("I'm positive")
default:
  fmt.Println("I'm NOT positive")
}
```

14.12. Continue Statements

A `continue` statement (without a label argument) begins the next iteration of the innermost `for` loop within the same function.

For example,

```
for i := range lines {
    if i % 2 == 0 {
        continue
    } else {
        println("An odd number")
    }
```

```
    }
```

The `continue` statement can be used with a label as a target (within the same function). In such a case, the `continue` statement transfers control to the labeled statement with the given label.

14.13. Break Statements

A `break` statement (without a label argument) terminates execution of the innermost compound statements, `for`, `switch`, or `select`, within the same function.

For example,

```
for i := range lines {
    if i > 10 {
        break
    } else {
        // the first (up to) 10 lines
        println(i)
    }
}
```

The `break` statement can be used with a label as a target, in which case it transfers control to the labeled statement with the given label.

14.14. Goto Statements

A `goto` statement consists of the keyword `goto` and a label that is defined elsewhere within the same function. The `goto` statement transfers control to the labeled statement with the given label.

```
func weirdFunc(isWeird bool) {
```

```
    if isWeird {
        goto Weird                               ①
    }
    return

Weird:
    fmt.println("Something weird happened.")      ②
}
```

① The `goto` statement syntactically requires a taget label, `Weird`, in this example.

② Note that the label `Weird` is declared in the scope of the `weirdFunc` function.

14.15. Defer Statements

A `defer` statement comprises:

- The `defer` keyword, followed by

- A (non-parenthesized) function or method call expression.

```
func doSomething() {
    defer cleanUp()
    doHeavyWork()
}
```

In this example, the `doHeavyWork` function is called first, and then before `doSomething` returns, `cleanUp` is called.

As with expression statements, certain builtin functions cannot be used in the `defer` statement.

When a `defer` statement executes in a function, the invocation of the given function/method is deferred until just before the enclosing function returns.

More precisely,

- Each time a "defer" statement executes,

  ◦ The function value and arguments to the call are evaluated and saved at the points of the statement execution, and

- Immediately before the enclosing function returns,

  ◦ All deferred functions are invoked, in the reverse order they were deferred, using saved values.

If the deferred function has any return values, then they are discarded. This behavior is the same as expression statements.

Note that, unlike the deferred function arguments, closed-over variables are evaluated at the point of the function call, and not at the point of the `defer` statement execution.

14.16. Return Statements

A `return` statement terminates the execution of the enclosing function, and it returns control to its calling function. The `return` statement can optionally provide one or more result values.

14.16.1. Functions without a result type

In a function declared without a result type, a `return` statement must not specify any result values.

```
func noResult() {
    return
}
```

14.16.2. Functions with a result type

In case of a function declared with a result type(s), the return value(s) may be explicitly specified in the `return` statement. For example,

```
func funcWithResultTypes() (int, int) {
    return 2, 10
}
```

When the function's result types specify the names of its parameters, then the return expression list may be omitted. The result parameters act as ordinary local variables. The simple `return` statement (without a trailing expression list) returns the values of these variables, as specified in the result parameter list.

```
func funcWithResultParameters2() (x, y int) {
    x, y = 0, 100
    return                          ①
}
```

① This `return` statement is equivalent to `return x, y`.

14.17. Go Statements

A go statement starts the execution of a function call in a separate goroutine, within the same address space.

Syntactically, the go statement is similar to the `defer` statement except that the keyword go is used instead of `defer`. That is, a go statement comprises:

- The go keyword, followed by
- A (non-parenthesized) function or method call expression.

14.17. Go Statements

For example,

```
go processSomething()
```

Goroutines are often used with channels.

Chapter 15. Errors

15.1. The `error` Interface

Programs may cause errors, during execution, in various parts of the code.

If a Go function, or a method, encounters an error, or an exceptional situation, which it cannot handle, it should return some sort of error indication to the caller.

The caller may be able to handle the error if it has enough contextual information. Or it may, in turn, decide to return an error indication to its own caller, through the call chain. By convention, Go functions typically return errors as one of their return values, often as the last one.

The Go language includes a predeclared `error` interface type:

```
type error interface {
    Error() string
}
```

Although it is not required, it is generally a good practice to use this common interface for representing an error condition. In this convention, the `nil` error value represents no error. When a non-`nil` error is returned, the normal return values are often ignored. When an error occurs, the function should just return the zero values for the normal return types.

As an example, a function for reading a file might be declared as follows:

```
func Read(f *File, b []byte) (n int, err error) {
    // f:    File handle
    // b:    bytes read from the file
    // n:    the number of bytes read
    // err:  error
    /* Implementation omitted */
}
```

When a non-nil err is returned, indicating an unexpected/exceptional condition, the normal return value n, which might be 0, should be ignored. In such a situation, the err value will describe what went wrong, which can be examined, e.g., using the error.Error method.

15.2. Run-Time Panics

Execution errors such as attempting to divide a number by 0, or trying to index an array beyond its legal bounds, trigger a run-time panic. This is equivalent to calling a builtin function panic with a value of the Error type from the runtime package.

15.2.1. The builtin panic function

When the error situation is so "severe" that the program execution cannot continue, we can use the builtin function panic. Calling panic, in effect, creates a run-time error which will bubble up the call chain and terminate the program (unless it is handled in some way).

The panic function takes one argument of any type. When the program terminates, the string value of that argument is printed to the stderr.

15.2.2. The builtin recover function

When the program panics, either through runtime errors or by an explicit call to the panic function, Go immediately stops execution of the current function of the current goroutine and begins unwinding the call stack.

In this process, all deferred functions are called. If any of the deferred functions, in this call chain, includes a call to the builtin recover function, then it stops the unwinding process and resumes the normal execution of the goroutine from that point on. The recover function returns the argument passed to the original panic.

This concludes the "reference" part of the book.

Chapter 16. Example Code (Bonus)

16.1. An Informal Introduction to Generics

Generics is *inherent* to the type systems of the statically and strongly typed languages whether a language officially supports it or not (e.g., Go pre-1.18 vs later).

For instance, as we briefly alluded in the earlier chapter, Go's builtin collection types, array, slice, map, and chan, are all generic types regardless of whether we call them such or not.

As an example, let's consider creating a series of int array types with the sizes 10, 11, 12, and more.

```
type intArr10 ... // Type for 10 element int arrays.
type intArr11 ... // Type for 11 element int arrays.
type intArr12 ... // Type for 12 element int arrays.
// ...
```

intArr10, intArr11, and intArr12 are all different and distinct types in Go, and yet they seem so similar to each other. The only difference is the number of elements in the array. It will be often too inconvenient to have to explicitly create a few dozens of, or even just a few, int array types this way. Go's builtin array literal syntax supports creating array types *parametrized* by their sizes.

```
type intArr10 [10]int
type intArr11 [11]int
type intArr12 [12]int
```

```
// ...
```

This example is a little bit convoluted, but the point is that we do not always have to create multiple types like `intArr10`, `intArr11`, and `intArr12`. Go's builtin syntax `[N]int` supports creating this (possibly infinite) series of *related types*, e.g., `[10]int`, `[11]int`, `[1000]int`, etc. (with `N == 10`, `N == 11`, `N == 1000`. etc.). *That is generics.*

Go allows creating array types with different element types as well. Syntactically, we can (unofficially) write it as `[N]T` where `T` stands for an arbitrary type. Note that a "generic type" like `[100]T` is now *parametrized by another type,* namely, its element type. (It represents a set of 100-element array types with their element type `T`.) Go's (new) generic type, or a parameterized type (parametrized by another type), uses different syntax, but the idea is the same.

A "generic type" defines a set of related (real/concrete) types. Despite the name, a generic type is not a "real type". It is like a template for real/concrete types. For example, you cannot use the `map` type directly in a Go program. You can only use concrete types like `map[int]string`. Go's built-in "map generic type" can be syntactically denoted as `map[K]V`, again unofficially, where `K` and `V` represent key and value types, respectively.

The syntactic difference can be a bit confusing, but unlike the builtin collection types, Go allows creating a generic type, and a generic function (that is, a function that uses generic types for its arguments and/or return values), using the special generic type syntax.

In case of the generic types, a generic type can be created using the named type definition syntax:

```
type TypeName[T1 Constraint1, T2 Constraint2, ...] AnotherType
```

Here, `AnotherType` can be a named or anonymous type such as a `struct` or `interface` type, which can depend on the generic type parameters, e.g., T1, T2, etc.

In case of the generic functions, a function that relies on a generic type can be created using the generic function declaration syntax:

```
func FunctionName[T1 Constraint1, T2 Constraint2, ...]
  (/* InputParameterList */)
  /* ReturnParameterList */
{
  // Function body statement list
}
```

In a generic function declaration, the *InputParameterList* and/or *ReturnParameterList* can include generic type parameters, e.g., T1, T2, etc. in place of the real/concrete types. Likewise, the function body can use the type parameters as if they are real, concrete types, as long as the implementation is consistent with their type constraints.

A few things to note:

- A container type is, by definition, a parametrized type. A container includes elements (of a particular type). Container types are the simplest, and the most important, use cases of generics.

- The type parameter constraint is always needed in Go's generics syntax even if it is just `any`.

- Note that in the builtin `map` types, the key values must be "hashable". This constraint is implicit. On the other hand, if we define a custom map/dictionary generic type, we can explicitly specify this requirement (at least in theory).

- Currently, as of Go 1.19, only two interfaces, `any` and `comparable`, are built into the language. It is expected that more interfaces (that can be used as type constraints) will be included in the standard library in the near future.

- Go's generics is somewhat limited, in various respects. For example, you cannot define a generic type that relies on integer values (e.g., like the builtin array types).

16.2. A Generic Stack

As an exercise, let's try and implement a *stack*. A stack is a container type that supports two operations, at a minimum:

- A method to add an element to the given container, typically called add, push, etc., and

- A method to take an element out of the container, typically called remove, pop, etc.

In addition, the remove/pop operation should remove the elements in the reverse order that they were added/pushed. This is called FILO, that is, First In - Last Out, or LIFO, Last In - First Out. This property *defines* the stack abstract data type.

A stack can be implemented in many different ways, including using Go's builtin slice. In this example, we will use a linked list data structure, for illustration.

16.2.1. Workspace setup

First, let's create a go module for our "stack library".

```
$ mkdir stack-demo && cd $_                              ①
$ mkdir stack && cd $_                                   ②
$ go mod init gitlab.com/.../stack-demo/stack            ③
$ cd ..                                                  ④
```

① stack-demo is our project folder. $_ refers to the last argument used in BASH.

② The stack library's module folder.

③ The full path is omitted, as indicated by .... The *go mod init* command creates a new *go.mod* file in the current directory.

④ At this point, we are back in the *stack-demo* directory (under some unspecified parent folder/path).

Although it is not really necessary for a simple project like this, we will create a separate module fo the "driver/test" program, e.g., for practice, and we will use the go workspace to manage these two modules.

```
$ go mod init gitlab.com/.../stack-demo                    ①
$ go mod edit -require \
               gitlab.com/.../stack-demo/stack@v0.1.0      ②
$ go mod edit -replace \
               gitlab.com/.../stack-demo/stack=./stack     ③
$ go work init                                             ④
$ go work use stack                                        ⑤
$ go work use .
```

① Although a go module roughly corresponds to a directory hierarchy with the *go.mod* file in its root/top directory, go modules need not be created in mutually exclusive locations. For illustration, we are creating this new module in the parent directory of the stack module.

② The `go mod edit -require` command is used to specify the module dependencies.

③ This is a common practice during the development so that the local files are used, which are presumably more up-to-date, rather than the ones already pushed to the remote repository.

④ A go workspace does not have to be created in a particular location, e.g., relative to its modules, as explained in the beginning of the book. But the project directory (which includes other modules, for instance) is often a good choice, if feasible. In this example, the workspace and the driver module are located in the same folder.

⑤ The *go work use* command is used to add modules to the given workspace. In this example, we add *stack* (a relative path under ... /stack-demo) for the `stack` library and . (.../stack-demo) for the driver program.

At this point, the project directory may look like this:

```
$ tree .                              ①
.
├── go.mod
├── go.work
└── stack
    └── go.mod

1 directory, 3 files
```

① *tree* is a Unix/Linux shell command that lists contents of directories in a tree-like format.

The *go.work* file:

```
go 1.19

use (
    ./
    ./stack                          ①
)
```

① Note that it is specified as *./stack*, not just as *stack*. It is beyond the scope of this book, but just as a note, you will need to pay attention to this kind of conventions when you use the modern *go* toolchain. It should be noted, among other things, that the GOROOT and GOPATH environment variables are (still) used by the *go* command.

The *go.mod* file for the driver module:

```
module gitlab.com/.../stack-demo                          ①

go 1.19

require gitlab.com/.../stack-demo/stack v0.1.0            ②
replace gitlab.com/.../stack-demo/stack => ./stack        ③
```

① "..." is not a valid syntax for the module path/name.

② This line is the result of running the *go mod edit -require* command, as illustrated above. It is not necessary to always use the *go* commands. You can manually edit the *go.work* and *go.mod* files.

③ Ditto. This is the result of running the *go mod edit -replace* command.

The *go.mod* file for the `stack` library module:

```
module gitlab.com/.../stack-demo/stack

go 1.19
```

16.2.2. The `stack` library

Now that we are done with the "administrative" task, let's start working on our `stack` library. First, let's define a generic `stack` type.

stack-demo/stack/stack.go

```
package stack                                             ①

type Pusher[E any] interface {                            ②
    Push(item E)
}

type Popper[E any] interface {                            ③
```

```
    PopOrError() (E, error)
}

type Stack[E any] interface {                    ④
    Pusher[E]
    Popper[E]
}
```

① By convention, the name of the package for the source files in ...
/stack-demo/stack is chosen to be `stack`, the last path segment.

② This generic `Pusher[E any]` interface includes one generic function
`Push(item E)`. It is also a convention to name a single-method
interface with the `er` suffix, e.g., `Pusher` for `Push` in this example.

③ In Go, unlike in some other languages, it is idiomatic to use many
small interfaces, e.g., rather than (more complete) big interfaces
with many methods. This generic `Popper` interface includes one
method `PopOrError() (E, error)`.

④ We do not have to define a `Stack` type. For illustration, we define
`Stack` as a combination of `Pusher` and `Popper` in this example,
using the interface embedding syntax. In fact, we do not even have
to explicitly define `Pusher` and `Popper` interfaces in this simple
example. See below.

 As stated, a stack type includes push and pop methods.
But, that is *not* the definition. The LIFO property is
essential in defining a stack. Note, however, that there
is no simple way to specify this requirement using the
language constructs like interfaces, not just in Go, but
in any other programming languages.

Now let's implement a linked list [https://en.wikipedia.org/wiki/Linked_list].

stack-demo/stack/node.go

```
package stack

type node[E any] struct {          ①
    item E
    next *node[E]                  ②
}
```

① A (non-exported) generic struct type named node.

② A field of a pointer type that points to the "next node", if any.

stack-demo/stack/linked-list.go

```
package stack

type list[E any] struct {                       ①
    head *node[E]
}

func newList[E any]() *list[E] {                 ②
    return &list[E]{
        head: nil,                               ③
    }
}

func (l *list[E]) addToHead(n *node[E]) {  ④
    n.next = l.head
    l.head = n
}

func (l *list[E]) removeHead() (n *node[E]) {
    n = l.head
    if n == nil {                                ⑤
        return
    }
    l.head = l.head.next
    return
```

```
    }
```

① A separate type for a linked list is not generally needed. One can just use node for a linked list.

② A function that returns an instance of a type is often called " constructors". They are conventionally named as "New" or some phrase that starts with "New" such as NewRocket (e.g., for a type named Rocket).

③ The zero value of a pointer type (e.g., *node[E] in this example) is nil. We use nil to represent "no head", or "no node" more generally.

④ A (singly) linked list type supports two main operations, among others. Adding a node to the head of the list, and removing the head node and resetting the head, called addToHead and removeHead in this example, respectively.

⑤ We just return a nil value when there is no head node to remove. This is just one API design. We could have used an extra return value of the error interface type, for instance, to indicate the empty list situation.

Now let's create a type that "implements the Stack interface", using the linkedList data structure that we just created.

stack-demo/stack/liststack.go

```
package stack

import (
    "errors"
    "fmt"
)

type ListStack[E any] struct {          ①
    *list[E]
}
```

```
func New[E any]() *ListStack[E] {              ②
    s := ListStack[E]{
        list: newList[E](),
    }
    return &s
}

func (s *ListStack[E]) Push(item E) {          ③
    n := node[E]{
        item: item,
    }
    s.addToHead(&n)
}

func (s *ListStack[E]) PopOrError()
    (E, error) {                               ④
    n := s.removeHead()
    if n == nil {
        var e E                                ⑤
        return e, errors.New("Empty list")
    }
    return n.item, nil
}
```

① We call this generic type ListStack, an arbitrary name.

② A constructor function, for illustration. Constructor functions are not normally needed for simple types. One can just use the composite literal syntax to create a new value.

③ Note the "generic method" syntax. The type parameter (e.g., E in this example) is associated with the method receiver (e.g., s for the *ListStack[E] type in this example).

④ The same with the PopOrError method. Note that the Pusher's PopOrError method return an "error" when the stack is empty.

⑤ It should be noted that Go does not (yet) have a syntax for creating the default or zero value for a type. This var declaration statement initializes the variable e with the zero value of type E (whatever the concrete type happens to be). We just use this e variable for a placeholder when we return an error.

Note that there is no reference of Pusher or Popper interfaces in this code. Go is rather unique in this regards. As explained earlier, a type *implicitly* implements an interface, by implementing relevant methods.

In this example, we did not even have to define explicit Pusher and Popper interfaces to define a type that implements these (possibly non-existing, implicit) interfaces. An explicit interface definition is needed when we *use the type* that implements the interface, e.g., as a function parameter, etc. For instance,

```
func PushToStack[E any](s Pusher[E], items ...E) {   ①
    for _, e := range items {
        s.Push(e)                                     ②
    }
}
```

① An explicit interface is needed here. Note that we just use Pusher[E] instead of Stack[E]...

② because the Push method is all that we need for the implementation of this function, PushToStack. Note that, in this example, the type parameter can be inferred and we do not have to write it as s.Push[E](e).

Just as a side note, this function can also be declared as follows:

```
func PushToStack[E any, S Pusher[E]](s S, items ...E) {
    // ...
}
```

Although these two function declarations are (obviously) different, they are nonetheless roughly equivalent. This is generally true for basic interfaces. They can be used as generic function type parameter constraints or simply as function parameters, with more or less the same effect. *Are the two usages really equivalent? Is there a reason why you would prefer one form to another? If so, in what situations?* We will leave this to the reader as something to think about while learning/programming in Go. (Hint: There are no "correct" answers.)

Another exercise, if you will, is to write a unit test for this ListStack[E] type. You can refer to the official doc, Go testing package [https://pkg.go.dev/testing], if you are new to unit testing in Go.

16.2.3. The driver program

Finally, here's the main function for simple testing:

stack-demo/main.go

```
package main

import (
    "fmt"

    "gitlab.com/.../stack-demo/stack"
)

func main() {
    lStack := stack.New[int]()                          ①

    lStack.Push(1)                                      ②
    lStack.Push(2)
    lStack.Push(3)
    fmt.Printf("Original Stack = %s\n", lStack)         ③

    for {                                               ④
        if item, err := lStack.PopOrError(); err == nil { ⑤
            fmt.Printf("Popped Item = %v\n", item)
            fmt.Printf("Current Stack = %s\n", lStack)
```

```
        } else {
            break                                           ⑥
        }
    }
}
```

① Since the type parameter cannot be inferred in this case (e.g., no initial values), it needs to be explicitly specified. In this example, we are creating a stack of int elements. That is, the type of lStack is *ListStack[int].

② Now that we can only push the elements of the int type to this stack, the type parameter need not be specified.

③ For the print functions to work effectively, ListStack[E], or its pointer type, will need to implement the fmt.Stringer interface. We will leave it as an exercise.

④ The infinite for loop.

⑤ The if statement. Note the simple statement before the Boolean condition.

⑥ The break statement. If the stack becomes empty, we stop the for loop.

16.3. Exercises

1. Implement a generic sorting function, e.g., using the quick-sort algorithm.

2. Create a generic queue type. A queue is a collection with the FIFO requirement, First-In First-Out.

3. Create a generic "sorted list" type, which supports adding/removing elements, and (zero-based) indexing. Indexing the n'th element returns the n'th "smallest" element, if any.

4. Implement a generic binary tree data structure. A binary tree

consists of a root node and its children (and, their children, etc.). Each node can have up to 2 children.

5. Implement a generic multi-map. A multi-map is a map/dictionary type in which there can be more than one elements with the same key.

Index

conversion expression, 99
Conversion of constant values, 99
Conversions, 90, 99
Converting, 90
coroutines, 125
corresponding key, 91
corresponding pointer type, 49
curly braces, 38, 72
current directory, 139

receiver type of a method, 54
receivers, 49
receiver's base type definition, 85
receiver's type, 86
receiver's value, 84
recover function, 134
redeclaration, 46
redeclared, 45
reference semantics, 69
regular assignment operator, 45
regular identifier, 39
related constants, 43
related Go packages, 24
related packages, 24
Relational operators, 101
Remainder, 103
remote git repositories, 28
remote repository, 139
remote source code repository, 17
repeated execution, 115
replace directive, 28
replace directives, 29
require directive, 28
result parameter list, 130
result parameters, 81, 130
result type, 97, 129
result types, 79
result values, 129
resulting slice, 63
return expression list, 130
return parameters, 98
return statement, 129-130
Return Statements, 129
return value, 100

return value types, 79
return values, 129
return variable, 39
Right shift, 103
right-hand expression, 109, 112
root directory, 24, 28
root node, 149
run time, 44, 64, 72
run-time error, 133
run-time panic, 64, 100, 105, 133
Run-Time Panics, 133
rune, 34
rune literal, 34-35
Rune literals, 34
rune literals, 36
runnable program, 19
runtime errors, 133
runtime package, 133
runtime panic, 100
runtime type, 123

S

scope, 37-39
scope of a constant, 39
scope of a type identifier, 39
scope of an identifier, 38-39
scope of an imported package name, 39
Scoping, 38
scoping, 39
select statement, 123-125
Select Statements, 123
Selector, 89
selector expression, 96
Selectors, 96

source files of a `package`, 14

source text, 38

special entry function, 18

special `main` package, 18

specified range, 95

square brackets, 54, 59, 61, 91

stack, 138

stack abstract data type, 138

stack frame, 83

`stack` library, 141

stack library, 138

standard arithmetic operators, 102

standard *go* build tool chain, 17

standard go toolchain, 14

statement, 114

statement context, 112

Statements, 38, 107

statements, 30, 102

statements in Go, 107

static type, 44, 48, 72, 99

string, 35, 99

String addition, 103

String concatenation, 103

string concatenation, 58

string constants, 42

string literal, 30

string literal syntax, 58

string literal tag, 71

String literals, 35

string literals, 35

`String` method, 78

string slice expressions, 95

string type, 99

String types, 57

string value, 57

string values, 57

Strings, 103

strings, 89

`struct`, 69, 137

struct definition, 53

struct literal, 91

Struct tags, 99

struct type, 46, 70

Struct Types, 69

struct types, 99

struct with no fields, 70

structs, 70

substring, 94

Substrings, 94

successive digits, 33

Sum, 102

surrounding function, 82-83

`switch` expression, 119-120, 122

switch expression, 120, 122

`switch` or `select` statement, 38

`switch` statement, 119, 121, 123

Switch Statements, 119

`switch` statements, 120, 124

syntactic error, 39

syntax, 45, 58, 84, 95-96, 120, 122-123

syntax of `interface`, 77

syntax ~T, 72

T

T itself, 72

Tags, 71

terminating statement, 81

the element type of the channel, 105

variadic, 79
variadic function, 62
Variadic functions, 79
versioning, 24

W

working directory, 25
workspace, 29, 140
workspace mode, 25
Workspace setup, 138
workspaces, 29

Z

zero value, 44, 59, 72, 100, 144-146
zero value of a `chan` type, 67
zero value of the `bool` type, 62
zero value of type, 46
Zero values, 21
zero values, 21, 132
zeroed slice structure, 47
zeroed storage, 46

About the Author

Harry Yoon has been programming for over three decades. He has used over 20 different programming languages in his professional career. His experience spans from scientific programming and machine learning to enterprise software and Web and mobile app development.

You can reach him via email: harry@codingbookspress.com.

He occasionally hangs out on social media as well:

- TikTok: @codeandtips [https://tiktok.com/@codeandtips]
- Instagram: @codeandtips [https://www.instagram.com/codeandtips/]
- Facebook Group: Code and Tips [https://www.facebook.com/groups/codeandtips]
- Twitter: @codeandtips [https://twitter.com/codeandtips]

Other Go Programming Books by the Author

- The Art of Go - Basics: Introduction to Programming in Golang - Beginner to Intermediate [https://www.amazon.com/dp/B08WYNG6YP]

About the Series

We are creating a number of books under the series title, *A Hitchhiker's Guide to the Modern Programming Languages*. We cover essential syntax of the 12 select languages in 100 pages or so, Go, C#, Python, Typescript, Rust, C++, Java, Julia, Javascript, Haskell, Scala, and Lua.

These are all very interesting and widely used languages that can teach you different ways of programming, and more importantly, different ways of thinking.

All Books in the Series

- Go Mini Reference [https://www.amazon.com/dp/B09V5QXTCC/]

- Modern C# Mini Reference [https://www.amazon.com/dp/B0B57PXLFC/]

- Python Mini Reference [https://www.amazon.com/dp/B0B2QJD6P8/]

- Typescript Mini Reference [https://www.amazon.com/dp/B0B54537JK/]

- Rust Mini Reference [https://www.amazon.com/dp/B09Y74PH2B/]

- C++20 Mini Reference [https://www.amazon.com/dp/B0B5YLXLB3/]

- Modern Java Mini Reference [https://www.amazon.com/dp/B0B75PCHW2/]

- Julia Mini Reference [https://www.amazon.com/dp/B0B6PZ2BCJ/]

- Javascript Mini Reference [https://www.amazon.com/dp/B0B75RZLRB/]

- Haskell Mini Reference [https://www.amazon.com/dp/B09X8PLG9P/]

- Scala 3 Mini Reference [https://www.amazon.com/dp/B0B95Y6584/]

- Lua Mini Reference [https://www.amazon.com/dp/B09V95T452/]

Community Support

Code and Tips

We are building a website for programmers, from beginners to more experienced. It covers various coding-related topics from algorithms to machine learning, and from design patterns to cybersecurity, and more. We publish new content on a weekly basis.

- www.codeandtips.com

You can also find some sample code in the GitLab repositories:

- gitlab.com/codeandtips

Mailing List

Please join our mailing list, join@codingbookspress.com, to receive coding tips and other news from **Coding Books Press**, including free, or discounted, book promotions. If you let us know which book you have bought, and if we find any significant errors in the book, then we will notify you. Advance review copies will be made available to select members on the list before new books are published so that their input can be incorporated, if feasible.

Office Hours

We may set up a regular time, weekly or monthly, to answer any questions from the readers, or to go through some of the exercises in the book together, *if there is a demand.* If you sign up on the mailing list, then we will notify you when the office hours starts.

Printed in Great Britain
by Amazon

14364760R00099